mobilized

Thank you for joining us tonight !

Enjoy getting

SC

mobilized

An insider's guide to the business and future of connected technology

SC Moatti

BK

Berrett–Koehler Publishers, Inc.
a BK Business book

Berrett-Koehler Publishers, Inc.
1333 Broadway, Suite 1000
Oakland, CA 94612-1921
Tel: (510) 817-2277   Fax: (510) 817-2278   www.bkconnection.com

Ordering Information

Quantity sales. Special discounts are available on quantity purchases by corporations, associations, and others. For details, contact the "Special Sales Department" at the Berrett-Koehler address above.

Individual sales. Berrett-Koehler publications are available through most bookstores. They can also be ordered directly from Berrett-Koehler:
Tel: (800) 929-2929; Fax: (802) 864-7626; www.bkconnection.com

Orders for college textbook/course adoption use. Please contact Berrett-Koehler:
Tel: (800) 929-2929; Fax: (802) 864-7626.

Orders by U.S. trade bookstores and wholesalers. Please contact Ingram Publisher Services, Tel: (800) 509-4887; Fax: (800) 838-1149; E-mail: customer. service@ingrampublisherservices.com; or visit www.ingrampublisherservices .com/Ordering for details about electronic ordering.

Berrett-Koehler and the BK logo are registered trademarks of Berrett-Koehler Publishers, Inc.

Printed in the United States of America

Berrett-Koehler books are printed on long-lasting acid-free paper. When it is available, we choose paper that has been manufactured by environmentally responsible processes. These may include using trees grown in sustainable forests, incorporating recycled paper, minimizing chlorine in bleaching, or recycling the energy produced at the paper mill.

Library of Congress Cataloging-in-Publication Data

Names: Moatti, S. C., author.
Title: Mobilized : an insider's guide to the business and future of connected
    technology / S.C. Moatti.
Description: First edition. | Oakland, CA : Berrett-Koehler Publishers, [2016] |
Includes bibliographical references and index.
Identifiers: LCCN 2015049231 | ISBN 9781626567405 (hardcover : alk. paper)
Subjects: LCSH: Mobile commerce. | Mobile communication systems.
    Technological innovations--Management.
Classification: LCC HF5548.34 .M623 2016 | DDC 658.8/72--dc23
LC record available at http://lccn.loc.gov/2015049231

First Edition

21 20 19 18 17 16   10 9 8 7 6 5 4 3 2 1

Project management and interior design by Dovetail Publishing Services
Cover design and production by Ran Lui and Dan Tesser

To Louise

Contents

Foreword *by Nir Eyal*   ix

Introduction
Experiencing the Mobile Revolution Firsthand   1

One   The New Gold Rush   13

Two   The Body Rule
The Best Mobile Products Operate by Beauty   39

Three   The Spirit Rule:
The Best Mobile Products Give Us Meaning   67

Four   The Mind Rule:
The Best Mobile Products Learn as We Use Them   91

Five   The Mobile Formula
In the Past, Present, and Future   121

Conclusion
It's Your Turn Now   147

Notes   153

Acknowledgments   163

Index   167

About the Author   173

Foreword
by Nir Eyal

I remember the first time I saw a URL. It was 1995, I was a teenager, and I was flipping through my hometown newspaper when I spotted a movie ad. At the bottom were the words "Check us out online at www . . ."

I had no idea what "www" meant, but being the nerd I was (and still am), I rushed to my computer. Eagerly, I waited 5 minutes for the spinning disks to boot up and weathered another 10 minutes of crashes and reboots.

Finally, I was able to type the URL into my Internet service provider's search bar, and Prodigy promptly took me nowhere. Instead of a web page, I got an error message.

Not that it would have mattered much.

Let me remind you that 1995 web pages were truly terrible. A look back at websites of yesteryear reveals hard-to-navigate, text-laden walls of words that no one would want to interact with today.

No wonder relatively few offline businesses shifted their resources into building an online presence. It would take years, if not a decade, after the first web browser was born for businesses to realize the importance of that lowly "www."

Today, having a website is a requirement—it's the modern-day equivalent of hanging a shingle, announcing you are open for business.

The lesson here is that—at first—sweeping industry changes can easily be dismissed. They're often seen as something companies can get to later on, when time allows and budgets free up. But, of course, later on often comes too late and, while laggards are still deciding what to do, their competitors are cashing in.

As of this writing in late 2015, we're just seven years into the mobile revolution as marked by the opening of the Apple App Store in 2008—and yet what an incredibly rapid revolution it has been.

Consider this: whereas most companies just a decade ago lacked even a basic mobile presence, today entire multibillion-dollar enterprises operate only in the mobile space. In fact, many of the biggest players and service providers globally—such as Uber—only exist in mobile.

Like so many did when websites first arrived, small and medium-sized businesses today have ignored or neglected their mobile strategy. However, giving customers a way to do business with you through their mobile devices is fast becoming a necessity, as important as having a presence on the World Wide Web. Just as eagerly as I wanted to get online as a teenager to check out that particular movie's website, your customers want to interact with you through their mobile devices. CNN reported last year that over half of Internet usage comes from mobile devices in the US—a percentage that is significantly higher in other parts of the world where mobile is the only way to access the web.[1]

In this book, my friend Sophie-Charlotte (SC) Moatti gets you ready for what's to come.

I first met SC three years ago. She was working at Facebook and invited me to speak to her team. I was impressed. "I'm going mobile only," she told me. "Trying to get my work done without a computer. I'm almost there . . ." When everyone else was still carrying around a laptop, SC was pioneering the effective use of mobile technology in ways the rest of us had yet to see.

SC recognizes the vital role mobile applications will play in our future. From her years of practice in mobile, she honed her craft and learned how to build mobile services and apps that get users engaged and keep them coming back.

In this book, she lays out the ground rules for what works and what doesn't in mobile. She shares insights she gleaned working at Facebook, Nokia, and other companies to give us her unique perspective on how to, in her words, "build products that count."

Enjoy getting mobilized!

mobilized

Introduction

Experiencing the Mobile Revolution Firsthand

Mobile has eaten the world.[2,3]

It's a technology that has greater power than most of the technologies that came before it. What's more, its power is only going to grow stronger, its reach into our lives deeper.

In this book, I am going to explain how mobile came to be, what makes the best mobile products, and how these factors influence the present and future of the industry.

To begin, let's talk about where mobile gets its power and how I became interested in it.

Most of us have a fairly simple way to keep technology at bay when we want to distance ourselves from it: we walk away. We leave the office or factory at the end of the work-day, we turn off the computer, we switch off the TV. . . .

But what of mobile products? Do we walk away from them the way we disconnect from most technology?

We hope we can simply turn off our smartphones, but very few of us do. In fact, statistics show that two people out of three place their mobile devices on the nightstand next to their bed.[4] It's the last thing we put down before we go to sleep and the first thing we check when we wake up.

We're not being forced to sleep with our mobile devices within arm's reach. We want to do it. We don't want to be separated from it. It's become what's called a *sticky* technology, where we've formed such a strong attachment to our mobile devices that our use of them is an ongoing, almost unconscious habit.

What if instead of a smartphone, our favorite mobile device was a watch? An earpiece? A pair of contact lenses? A smart patch? A smart pill? A digital nerve ending? As mobile devices shrink, they get more and more integrated into everyday objects around us and more and more deeply embedded within us.

The mobile revolution isn't simply a technological invention from which we can disconnect at any time. We can't disengage from the air we breathe or from the feet that carry us. Similarly, in today's world we can't disconnect from our mobile products.

Our mobile products are new extensions of ourselves.[5] What we should expect from them is what we wish for ourselves: an attractive body, a meaningful life, and becoming smarter about the things that count. This is the foundation behind successful mobile products.

꩜ ꩜ ꩜

To begin, let me tell you how I got involved in mobile and how my views about it were shaped.

For most of my professional life, I've helped companies become mobile. I've launched and monetized mobile products that are used by billions of people.

In 2007, I was part of a team of Stanford graduates who joined the incubation labs of Nokia. When it came to mobile, Nokia was the undisputed market leader. Our mission was to build a service that helped users discover information about an object or a location simply by pointing their phone at it. Within less than two years, our team grew from 3 to more than 70 people. Millions of customers downloaded our app. The press gave us some really nice reviews.

Soon, it reached the top 1 percent of the app store and received coveted industry awards, including an International Digital Emmy nomination and *WSJ* Innovator runner-up.[6] In fact, it was so successful that Nokia decided to preinstall it on every one of its smartphones. It was a big deal for our small team.

At the time, two out of every five smartphones were sold by Nokia. The company was so successful at it, in fact, that several of its competitors, mobile manufacturers like Samsung and Motorola, were headed toward bankruptcy. Meanwhile, recognizing the implications of Nokia's success, a few Silicon Valley staples were radically changing their strategy to become mobile.

This was really exciting, but at first I didn't get it. Why would blue chips like Apple and Google put their entire business at risk to enter a market that was so quickly consolidating?

I wanted to find the answer, so I embarked on a journey to understand how companies and people would become successful in this new mobile age. How would mobile start-ups make their mark in a world ruled by giant phone manufacturers and operators that strictly controlled access to their online content and services? What would happen when incumbents placed their bets and consolidated? And more importantly, what did that mean for me, you, and all our friends and colleagues? How would the mobile revolution affect our careers and our lives?

I looked for a formula that would help me navigate the mobile revolution. To my disappointment, I found none. Successful mobile insiders guarded their successes and secrets, and although I uncovered books, white papers, and blog posts, they at best only scratched the surface.[7] There was no guide for making sense of the burgeoning mobile industry.

In 2010, I left Nokia and started my own mobile company. I worked days and nights with an awesome team of pioneers in our tiny office in SoMa, the start-up neighborhood of San Francisco. We set out to build a product that would capture mobile's essence, one that would connect people and be super-contextual and personalized.

We came up with a few ideas that fit these criteria and, after some trial and error, decided on one: dating. We then refined the idea, figuring that the best way to meet someone is to be set up by friends. So we developed the product to match friends of friends who were nearby one another and whom we thought could be a romantic match.

Soon after we launched, we found a passionate group of loyal users. On our mobile app, they could browse through thousands (eventually hundreds of thousands) of profiles and ask their friends for an opinion. It was simple and fun. It was hyper-personal and safe at the same time. We kept tweaking the experience based on what people liked.

We raised money from some of the smartest Silicon Valley insiders and piqued the interest of Facebook, the social networking giant. They liked the way we thought of mobile and offered to bring us in to help them figure out what they could make of the mobile revolution. We sold the company. I joined Facebook.

At Facebook, I worked with very bright and ambitious people to try and keep up with the company's exponential growth. They brought me in because of my experience building a mobile start-up, but the nature of the work at Facebook was completely different from what we did at a start-up. At my previous job, we were trying to discover what people would actually do with mobile. At Facebook, we knew what users wanted; our job was just to keep up with the incredible rise of the social network as it branched into mobile.

I loved the work we were doing at Facebook, but I decided to leave when Trulia, the real estate marketplace, offered me the opportunity to head up its rentals division. I found myself surprised again at how different this experience was from my previous ones, even though we were yet again driving the mobile revolution. Trulia's founder asked me to join precisely because of my work at both a mobile start-up and a hyper-growth company. But instead of developing our mobile product, my team and I focused most of our time and effort increasing mobile revenue and consolidating our projects to reduce cost.

In 2015, I was invited to serve on the board of directors of Opera Software, the global mobile browser and advertising network. I remembered the company as a market leader providing high-performing mobile browsers to Nokia and other phone manufacturers. When smartphones became mainstream, Opera completely reinvented itself. In only a few years, it became a market leader providing mobile video advertising across more than one billion mobile phones globally.

Despite my experience in several tech companies, I still could not wrap my head around the mobile revolution. Organizations big and small were rushing into it without thinking much about the consequences. Silicon Valley entrepreneurs were excited about using mobile to create new business models without much consideration for the impact it might have on society. Corporate America was in a hurry to launch apps at any cost without thinking about how mobile could be a source of additional revenue. Governments eagerly anticipated access to massive amounts of data that could help prevent terrorism without considering how it would limit citizens' freedoms.

It all felt random, and no one seemed to be defining the formula for mobile success. What was the nature of mobile and the essence of its impact on our lives? Beyond features and functions, business models and money, what was our vision for the mobile revolution?

I looked for insights from friends and colleagues, trying to uncover the rules behind great mobile products. I sought to identify the commonalities between the most successful ones and understand what the others were doing differently. In addition to managers and coworkers I had worked with at Facebook, Nokia, Opera, and Trulia, I spoke with executives at mobile pioneers, including Apple,

Amazon, Airbnb, Google, Instagram, GreenOwl, Lyft, MyFitnessPal, Pandora, Slack, Tinder, Uber, Viber, Yelp, Andreessen Horowitz, Autodesk, and others.

In 2013, I began blogging about what I learned at www.ProductsThatCount.com, and my essays were syndicated to such other sites as the Harvard Business Review and the Huffington Post. Soon, readers began sending me their own case studies, perspectives, and questions.

These years of experience and research finally resulted in the creation of the Mobile Formula, a set of three all-encompassing rules behind exceptional mobile products. The Mobile Formula is the backbone of this book.

Mobilized is for anyone who wants to participate in the mobile revolution, from recent college graduates to working professionals, serial entrepreneurs, and corporate leaders. Whether you have your own mobile start-up, work at a hyper-growth company, have a job at an established corporation, or are between projects, you will learn how to apply the Mobile Formula to your own circumstances. In the process, you will help build a more connected world by being a better-informed participant in the mobile revolution.

This book is also for anyone interested in cutting-edge technology, innovative marketing, artificial intelligence (AI), and how these and related fields intersect with human psychology, economics, and social movements. Mobile is an entrenched part of your life already (if not, it soon will be); this book will provide an insider's perspective into how that occurred.

I realize *mobilized* might seem like a book on technology, but really it's a book about us humans. Of course, we're going to look at technology and what makes for great mobile products. But if you only study the technology, you'll end up with an incomplete picture.

Why? Because the best mobile products are based on *human-first* principles. Great mobile products don't look inward, focusing soley on churning 1s and 0s; rather, they look out at the world and the people in it. Mobile doesn't rob us of our humanity; it amplifies it.

The Mobile Formula is about us, humans, and what matters to us. So in addition to the Facebooks and Ubers of the world, we're also going to look at such forward-thinking individuals as mathematician Pythagoras, author Leo Tolstoy, philosopher Martin Heidegger, and statesman Nelson Mandela to see how they went about finding answers to life's big questions.

Here is what lies ahead:

- Chapter 1 talks about how the mobile revolution is transforming the business world on all levels—technologically, economically, strategically, even culturally.

- Chapters 2, 3, and 4 describe the three components of the Mobile Formula. They look in detail at what the most successful companies are doing with mobile, and how mobile replicates human behavior and amplifies human experience.

◆ Chapter 5 examines how the Mobile Formula applies to past and current mobile products, and how we can use it to predict what future mobile products will do.

Throughout the book, I apply the Mobile Formula to case studies of companies that joined the mobile revolution—how they did it and how you can, too.

As you're reading, you'll find many references to Facebook. That's not just because much of what Facebook is doing in mobile is laudable, or because the mobile revolution is mostly about software, less about hardware. It's also because, since I worked there, I know how we made our choices. I'm not trying to push Facebook or their choices on you, though. In fact, I write about the intriguing choices made by several other Silicon Valley companies, including Airbnb and Pandora. All these familiar players are a big part of the evolving mobile story.

The Mobile Formula works in organizations of any size and ambition. But the specifics vary a lot, and this book provides ways to understand them and tailor them to your own situation. As you read, make notes about the specific aspects of your situation that require particular attention, and how the Mobile Formula could be applied to them.

At the beginning of each chapter, I provide a brief summary of the content to follow. I half-kiddingly title the boxes by the old Internet acronym TL;DR (Too Long; Didn't Read), but they are meant to set the stage for what you are about to read rather than give you an excuse not to read it!

At the end of each chapter, you'll find some key take-aways to focus on. Review them alone, discuss them with your team, and share them with your network. If you have questions, I'm here to help.

Chapter 1

The New Gold Rush

TL;DR **Too Long; Didn't Read**

- People spend more time on their mobile products than on their computers, so businesses are adjusting their strategy to focus more on mobile.

- In addition, entrepreneurs are creating new types of businesses: the sharing economy.

- This shift is much bigger than technology or marketing; it's about company culture.

- What guides the success of all mobile products—past, present, and future—is the Mobile Formula. It has three rules: the Body Rule, the Spirit Rule, and the Mind Rule.

Imagine for a moment that your phone bill is as high as your rent or mortgage. Would you be able to afford it? Would you cancel your smartphone plan? Would you move to a smaller and cheaper home so you could continue to pay for your phone?

In 2015, the Boston Consulting Group (BCG) published the results of a global survey showing that an average person puts an implied value of up to $6,000 on their smartphone, or more accurately on the apps that run on smartphones.[8] In developing countries like China and India, this represents 40 percent of average income.

That's the price some people are willing to pay for mobile apps. People care as much about their mobile products as they do where they live. It's that significant.

Today, mobile contributes about 5 percent of gross domestic product (GDP) in the countries surveyed by BCG (and as high as 11 percent in one country: South Korea) and represents almost 8 percent of all venture capital investment. Cumulatively, it's more than the GDP of every country in the world except for the United States and China.

Yet unlike other infrastructure investments of similar magnitude, such as energy and transportation networks, most of this investment is privately funded.

Mobile is about private wealth, not government programs.

So the mobile revolution has created a new gold rush, a Wild West environment where people are ambitious and opportunities are everywhere. I'm surprised every day to discover the extent to which it is creating unprecedented prosperity. Every business wants to and should get a meaningful piece of it.

Given this potential for profit, almost every company I speak with wants to become *mobile-first*. But what does that mean?

Where People Go, Business Follows

Since 2014, there have been more mobile devices in the world than desktop computers, and people spend more time browsing the Internet on their smartphones than on their desktops. So companies simply cannot ignore mobile as a channel to reach their consumers. But to be effective, mobile marketing requires dedicated mobile products such as smartphone apps. Let me explain.

Marketers who work at companies that do not have a mobile product have limited options to reach consumers on mobile. They can advertise on mobile, of course. In 2015, every other dollar spent on digital advertising was spent on mobile. They can also reach their consumers through mobile social networks like Facebook, Instagram, and Twitter, and mobile messengers like WhatsApp, Line, and WeChat. But without a mobile product, that's about all a mobile marketer can do. Their options are limited.

On the other hand, marketers who work at companies that have a mobile product such as a mobile-friendly website (also called a *responsive website*) have many more ways to reach their consumers. They can improve their ranking in search results on Google, which recently started to favor mobile-friendly websites in its search algorithm. They can create contextual offers, which are personalized to a user's time and place.

But that's still very limited, because when 9 out of 10 people spend their time in smartphone apps instead of in a mobile browser, a mobile website has significantly less reach than a smartphone app. On top of that, people who use a company's mobile app are generally better, more loyal customers than people who use its website.

Having a smartphone app allows marketers to take full advantage of what makes mobile unique and powerful as a way to reach people. They can, for instance, use free mobile distribution and promotion channels like app stores. They can send push notifications—messages sent ("pushed") to users without being specifically requested by users. They can negotiate with carriers to have their smartphone app preloaded so it will be widely distributed and promoted. They can use so-called multi-touch attribution tools that precisely measure the effectiveness of their campaigns across multiple channels.

"With mobile, we're moving from *Mad Men* to Math Men," says Sigal Bareket, founder and CEO of mobile performance advertising leader Taptica. "Everything is measurable and as a result, almost everything is predictable."

In the *Mad Men* era, it was almost impossible to track the effectiveness of advertising campaigns. Marketers were deemed "creative," which was a way to say that campaigns were sometimes successful, sometimes not, and that nobody really understood why.

Mobile marketers no longer rely on the hope that creative geniuses will whisper the right thing in the ears of people who look like they could become customers. Instead, they buy ROI (return on investment). They spend marketing dollars only if and when they get customers.

This emerging mobile performance advertising industry is helping mobile companies reach consumers in unprecedented ways. And because mobile products know a lot about their users, marketers are able to learn a lot about their customers and how to reach them. For instance, they can find out which ad in which app was the most popular among men aged 35–44 in New York City. That's a pretty valuable piece of information if this group represents your target customers, don't you think?

To illustrate what I'm saying, let's look at a hypothetical T-shirt company called TC. We'll see that while TC has limited options to reach its customers on mobile without a mobile product, having a mobile product gives TC a competitive advantage.

If TC doesn't have a mobile product, its alternatives on mobile are few: it can advertise, or get its customers to, say, share selfies on Instagram when they're wearing their T-shirts. But that's about it.

If it has a mobile website, TC no longer misses a sale because a shopper wanted to compare prices back home on the computer before buying. It also ranks higher on search results of people who look for T-shirts. It can show special offers to people who are in or near a mall where their T-shirts are sold. That's better, but still limited.

If it has a smartphone app, TC can get visibility for its brand and promotions through mobile app stores. It can send its customers push notifications to let them know about new arrivals or special offers. It can track all the steps a shopper goes through when buying: Did they look up a retail store once they knew which T-shirt they liked, or did they come to the store first? Did they compare prices? All of that, TC couldn't do before. But it gets even better: all of that, TC can do for free. It doesn't cost the company any advertising dollars.

As we see, having a mobile product provides lots of benefits for TC, including better targeting, more personalized promotions, stronger loyalty, and increased sales. It's a marketer's dream come true.

But having a smartphone app means that mobile is no longer only a marketing channel—it's also a product. That comes with sizeable cost implications. Let's examine this.

Launching a product on mobile isn't launching just one mobile product: it's launching an app for iPhone, an app for Android, and often a responsive website, an app for tablets, and an app for other mobile products like a smartwatch. According to mobile analytics firm Flurry, smartphone apps represent a $100 billion industry that's supported by $2 trillion in infrastructure investment.[9]

Because of that, many companies feel that mobile is a burden. A big cost with no return. Another one of those expensive IT projects. They hate the idea that they might need to hire mobile engineers. Mobile engineers are highly skilled and very rare, so they demand high salaries. These businesses don't think building a smartphone app is cool, let alone valuable. They know they must build one; they're just not sure why. On their profit and loss statements, they put smartphone apps in the loss section.

Meanwhile, they set out to cram their complex website to fit a small screen. Often, it's a painful exercise and the results aren't effective: poor user experience, crowded app stores, limited customer or business value.

During the dot-com era, many companies felt just the same about the Internet: it was a burden. Back then, many of them hurried to build websites that mirrored their paper catalogs.

If you're old enough, you probably remember some of these rigid websites. They had bare-bones site maps that looked like a table of contents. Clicking on a link would open a static web page with a lengthy product description, and sometimes a couple of pictures. And that was it. Visitors to the website couldn't read reviews, or go from one product to another to see what others had purchased, or compare prices, let alone buy online. So few of them came back to the site. It became a self-fulfilling prophecy that websites cost more than they yielded and that all they did was add new line items to already too fat IT budgets.

I'll let you in on a secret: if you use the same approach, you'll get the same results. It took over a decade for businesses to figure out the value of the Internet, from e-commerce services to search directories. If companies tackle mobile the same way they tackled the Internet, by building apps that look like websites, it's also going to take them years to find value in mobile. And they'll be left wondering: Do the benefits really outweigh the cost?

Let's go back to our earlier example, the T-shirt company TC. What would happen if it refused to build a mobile product and decided to ignore the mobile revolution? People obviously wouldn't stop buying clothes the way they stopped buying print photos or VCRs. So for a while, things would continue as they were.

Meanwhile, a lot of small companies would use mobile to try and meet the needs of consumers in ways TC wasn't. They might innovate in interesting ways. For instance, many smartphone apps today let people overlay T-shirts on a picture of themselves rather than having to try them on physically at a store. These apps made headlines recently because it's so much more efficient to shop for clothes this way. Other apps let people design their own T-shirt by drawing on the touch screen, using a variety of templates. People love to personalize clothes because they find it fun and unique. Soon enough, these custom T-shirts could be produced at people's home, using a 3-D printer.

This trend is known as *smart apparel,* and as these companies grow, they will find more and more ways for people to try on, design, and make their own T-shirts on the go. And it's all because they are utilizing mobile products that improve constantly and quickly to meet these new consumer expectations. If TC still ignores the mobile revolution by then, its business could be in jeopardy.

When we refuse to adapt, we become isolated, strategic thinking stagnates, and businesses go bankrupt.

Take Yahoo, the former search giant. The company was born in the early days of the Internet and quickly established itself as a leader in the emerging online advertising industry. Its search technology was a game changer. Its portals were extremely popular destinations. Its mobile offering, Yahoo Go, was by far the best one out there.

At the time, advertising was still in the *Mad Men* era. Advertisers paid ad agencies extraordinary amounts of money to come up with cool banners.

"We make our money from people being shown ads," said Yahoo founder Jerry Yang.[10]

Instead of disrupting that ecosystem with its search technology, something Google would do soon after, Yahoo embraced it and set out to become one of these old-school media companies. Inexplicably, the board was convinced that people would never get tired of ad banners. They thought search was a fad that would go away by itself and as a result, the company turned its back on the very thing that had made it successful in the first place.

As early as the 2007, people already felt that Yahoo wasn't keeping up. The company had four CEOs in one year. It reacted years later, by partnering with Internet giants like Google and Alibaba and by bringing on Google's heralded executive, Marissa Mayer, as CEO.

By then, the battle for search had been long lost to Google. The new battle was mobile. Mayer acted quickly, aggressively bringing in mobile talent through over 30 acquisitions. Unfortunately, it was also too late. Yahoo had lost its edge.

As I'm writing this in late 2015, Yahoo has put itself up for sale. The company refused to adapt. It wasn't able to recognize that behaviors had changed.

Denial is someone else's opportunity. In fact, the mobile revolution has created completely new types of businesses—darlings like ridesharing service Uber and local delivery service Postmates, which are part of the dynamic new *sharing economy*. These businesses could not exist without mobile, and they are worth exploring in some depth.

The New Entrepreneurs of the Sharing Economy

"The sharing economy is a peer-based movement that empowers individuals to get what they need from each other," says sharing economy expert Jeremiah Owyang.[11] "[It] stretches across many aspects of our lives and businesses." It's usually thought of as a way for some people to make extra cash by renting out an asset they already own, such as their home or car.

Sharing companies have exploded with the mobile revolution. Today, two out of three people participate in the sharing economy, either by sharing/renting out their own assets, or by renting the assets of others.[12]

Consider Postmates. It connects people with local couriers who purchase and deliver goods from any restaurant or store in a city. Postmates could not exist without mobile. Its couriers are constantly on the go and their itinerary is calculated, optimized, and delivered in real time. For instance, its system can predict how long it takes a restaurant to get a to-go meal ready. It takes this information into account when sending a courier so that they don't need to wait around to pick it up.

After a few trials in San Francisco and other cities, Postmates is expanding to 30+ metros in the US. It has done millions of deliveries. Its founder and CEO, Bastian Lehmann, calls the company the anti-Amazon.[13]

"Amazon comes along and builds a warehouse outside a city," he says. "We like to say the city's our warehouse. We try to understand the inventory available [and build] a fleet of delivery people that distribute this inventory."

As the sharing economy matures, it has become more professionalized.[14] Several entrepreneurs are setting themselves up as middlemen—what I call the power sharer, the power operator, and the power organizer—and they are creating social mobility and financial wealth.

The power sharer optimizes asset selection and utilization. In large cities, where there is lots of demand for services, they buy assets in order to rent them to participants in the sharing economy. Consider Breeze, a car-leasing service. For a membership fee and a weekly fee, they'll lease you a car you can use to fuel your own sharing economy employment, whether it's as a courier for Postmates, a driver for Lyft, or a shopper for Instacart (or all three). And unlike a traditional lease, you can cancel your car with just two weeks' notice.

The power operator empowers freelancers of the sharing economy with crucial tools. Many sharing economy services cater to a very large pool of people. Often, they have no idea how to run a business, nor the time or desire to learn. For instance, say you move for a job and decide that rather than selling your apartment, you'll rent it on Airbnb or HomeAway, the vacation rental marketplaces. If you really wanted to ramp up, you'd need tools to run your operation efficiently: the ability to screen all the applicants, make sure the apartment is cleaned between each guest, and so on. A company like Pillow will do that in exchange for a commission on rent generated via Airbnb.

The power organizer organizes community and builds trust. One current downside of the sharing economy is that each participant has to learn on their own what works and what doesn't. There's no manager talking about identifying the most profitable opportunities, no union talking about safety. There's a need for communities in which sharers exchange knowledge. Power organizer Peers.org provides a platform to organize, curate, educate, and moderate participants in the sharing economy.

Power sharers, operators, and organizers plug into a key component of the sharing economy: its flexibility.

The jobs of the sharing economy are very flexible. Postmates couriers and Uber drivers can pretty much work whenever they want and wherever current regulations allow. By making their services available whenever and wherever they're needed, the three power optimizers have become a "force multiplier" of the sharing economy, allowing the ground troops of the movement to better achieve their lifestyle and financial goals.

But here's the catch: today, most sharing economy gigs are about earning a supplemental income rather than a living wage. Ride-sharers for instance, don't think of themselves as drivers, but rather as musicians, artists, or stay-at-home moms who seek additional income to support their passions. And that needs to change if the sharing phenomenon is ever going to live up to its promise as a game-changing employment model.

I believe the jobs created by the entrepreneurs of the sharing economy will ultimately pay well. In fact, I see sharing as the new Fordism,[15] the term used to describe the economic engine of mass production and mass consumption that dominated the twentieth century. The sharing economy is to the services industry what Fordism is to manufacturing. Let me explain. In Fordism, products are ordinary, everyday items (cars, refrigerators); similarly in the sharing economy, services are ordinary (taxi rides, grocery delivery). In Fordism, products are assembled mostly by low-skilled workers in a standard, replicable manner; similarly in the sharing economy, services are performed mostly by low-skilled workers in a replicable manner.

Unlike Fordism, where workers were paid higher wages so they could afford to purchase the products they made, the sharing economy today underpays its workers. For instance, nearly three out of five ridesharing drivers earn less than $10,000 annually in driving income, so most are using it as a second or third job.[16]

Because their wages are too low, sharing workers generally can't afford the services they perform. As it is, it's hard to see how the sharing economy can sustain itself over the long term. But I believe this will soon change: sharing companies will need to raise their wages not only to attract the best workers in an increasingly competitive environment but to allow those workers to be their own customers. This is what will give birth to a new middle class.

So we've looked at the benefits of the mobile revolution, and how mobile products can transform the art and science of marketing to today's consumers. And we've seen how mobile has given birth to a dynamic new phenomenon: the sharing economy.

We've established that mobile is not just a new marketing channel, or a cool app, or an appendix. It's not a side dish; it's the main dish. It's the entrée. It's much more than simply hiring the right people to develop mobile products tailored toward an established product or service.

But if a company is new to this game (as many still are), how should it tackle mobile?

This is where culture comes in.

Becoming Mobile-First Is a Cultural Transformation

You may remember articles from a few years ago with headlines such as "Facebook Doesn't [Get] Mobile and That Spells Disaster."[17] At the time, the company thought that mobile was about technology, so it trained all its engineers in the new programming languages required to build smartphone apps.

"Technically, it was easy," says engineering executive and Silicon Valley veteran Jocelyn Goldfein, who led Facebook's mobile-first transition.[18]

The company set up a weeklong boot camp for all its engineers to help them learn mobile programming languages. But this approach didn't work. In fact, the stock went from $40 to $20 per share.

"The hard part was the change in culture," Goldfein admitted. "The only value we could all get behind is the experience of the user."

Before the mobile-first transition, one of Facebook's core values was "move fast and break things." Well, breaking a website can usually be fixed within a few hours, but breaking a smartphone app takes weeks to repair. Why? Because unlike websites, smartphone apps go through thorough quality controls before Apple or Google will release them. This can take weeks and once they're out, they go through another vetting process when they are reviewed and ranked by users.

Imagine the impact, on both users and the parent company, of an app that could be broken quickly and remain broken for weeks. There would be negative reviews, disengagement, lost sales, and more. When people discover they've invested time in a mobile product that doesn't work, they feel that their time is not being valued and they vent their frustration by no longer using the product.

It wasn't until it realized that transitioning to mobile is about culture more so than technology that Facebook truly became mobile-first. Only then did its stock go from $20 all the way to $80 per share.

To adapt to mobile, Facebook had to change its core value to "move fast" . . . but no more breaking things.

The company accelerated the culture change by making a number of talent acquisitions (including me) in order to bring in people with experience launching mobile products. And it made some major strategic acquisitions, including Instagram and WhatsApp. Now, Facebook has a portfolio of mobile products: Facebook, Instagram, WhatsApp, Oculus Rift, and more on the way.

This doesn't just apply to Facebook or Silicon Valley. It applies across the board. Whether businesses already have a mobile presence today or are just starting with mobile, whether they are part of the sharing economy or not, the single best way for them to succeed in mobile is to adapt their entire culture to become mobile.

This transformation is an opportunity for a business to rethink the way it serves its customers, to reinvent itself.[19] It means thinking about their company as a mobile service with a giant back office that does all the other things they do now. This isn't saying that they should get rid of their manufacturing plant or stores. This is saying that today's customers associate their company with their mobile service, not their plant or stores. It doesn't matter if they're a T-shirt company, car manufacturer, insurance provider, or department store. By becoming mobile-first, their former core focus will follow. And profitably.

Becoming mobile-first isn't just about technology. Harnessing the technology is important, of course, but it can be incredibly dense, technical, and hard to grasp for anyone but the most dedicated of technologists.

The truth is much simpler. It's about *knowing what makes us human*. That's what defines a culture, right?

Becoming mobile-first is about letting people be people both inside and outside organizations. It's about us as individuals. It's unlearning everything we learned from the industrial revolution about mass production and scale.

If you can understand this, you can understand the key to effective mobile products.

The Mobile Formula Follows Human-First Principles

Let's not think about mobile for a moment. Let's think about our lives. What do we love? What do we hate? What do we need help with?

Mind, body, spirit is a universal trilogy to help us consider these questions. Together, they encapsulate what it means to be human.

How does this relate to mobile? Let's consider each component of the trilogy, in a slightly different order.

- Body: We are guided and motivated by beauty in all pursuits—whether in a mate, in our dwellings or environments, in esthetics, and in the arts. Great mobile products replicate this beauty and use it to attract us. We appreciate beauty in two ways: aesthetically and by utility. An athlete's body is physically attractive, but the muscles, structure, and build all contribute to purpose and utility. It's the same with mobile. There were lots of music programs and software before iTunes, but none of them were as attractive and none were so simple and easy to use.

- Spirit: We all seek meaning for ourselves and our communities. Our spirit defines us and marks us as individuals. At the same time, we are each not just individuals; we are a part of larger groups. The best mobile products recognize this duality. They give us meaning as individuals by adapting to our wants, needs, and preferences in such a way that they become extensions of our spirit. Conversely, they recognize that our spirits work in the same space as other spirits, and with that there needs to be adequate accounting for manners, privacy, and other social norms.

◆ Mind: Key to our development as humans and our ongoing survival, both individually and collectively, is our ability to learn and adapt. Adaptability, said Darwin himself, is a matter of survival. The best mobile products not only help us learn but also learn with us. We learn over the course of our life through trial and error, through experience, through modifications and growth. Similarly, mobile products learn and adapt over time by reacting to and for their users.

These three human-first principles are at the core of great mobile products. Because they are extensions of ourselves, we expect from them what we wish for ourselves. We want them to look beautiful, to focus on the things that matter, and to constantly adapt to our environment. An attractive body, spiritual maturity, and a masterful mind.

Mind: **Learning**

Spirit: **Meaning**

Body: **Beauty**

The mind-body-spirit trilogy is the basis for the Mobile Formula, the three rules that guide all mobile products—past, present, and future:

- The Body Rule tells us how to create beautiful mobile products.

- The Spirit Rule explains how to make sure mobile products focus on the things that matter to us.

- The Mind Rule describes how mobile products effectively adapt to and survive in the constantly evolving mobile landscape.

These rules apply whether companies have already transitioned to mobile and seek to grow usage and revenue, or whether they are just getting started and looking for a blueprint to launch and create a positive user experience.

The Mobile Formula at a Glance

The rules of the Mobile Formula are grounded in the three essential elements within us: body, spirit, and mind.

The Body Rule

All successful mobile products are beautiful, but how to define their beauty? In mobile, beauty comes from two things: efficiency and what I call "wow."

Because of the small size of mobile products, nothing can be wasted. Mobile designers need to be efficient. They distill tasks and flows to their essence.

The visceral feeling we get when we see a beautiful mobile product skips our consciousness. Their beauty confounds us. Mobile designers need to build products that wow us in this way.

The Spirit Rule

One of the most disruptive aspects of mobile products is that they are with us always. To be successful, they need to understand what matters to us and help us get it. This comes through personalization and community.

The more mobile products know about us, the more personalized they become. They understand what matters to us as individuals with unique feelings and emotions. So people come to rely on them extensively and often become emotionally attached to them.

Mobile also helps us focus on what matters in our communities, where social rules and rituals are needed.

The Mind Rule

Mobile products must also constantly adapt. They become successful by learning both fast and slow.

On mobile, user behaviors and technology change at an incredibly rapid pace. Mobile companies understand that the more people use their product, the better it gets. They need to learn fast to adapt to changing expectations and conditions.

On the other hand, they also need to learn slow. They have no choice but to reinvent themselves over the long haul by reaching new users, launching new products, or inventing new business models.

We'll spend the next few chapters examining the rules of the Mobile Formula and how mobile-first pioneers apply them today. Then, we'll take a look at the Mobile Formula in the context of past, present, and future mobile products.

Remember and Share

◆ Today, every company knows that it needs to become mobile-first. The mobile revolution has created a new gold rush. It's fueled by the fact that people spend more time on their mobile products than on their computers.

• Increasingly, marketing departments are focusing their time and budget on mobile. But without a mobile product, their options are limited. Technology needs to be involved and as a result, many companies see mobile as a burden—yet another dreary IT project.

• For existing businesses, becoming mobile-first is really about changing company culture. Businesses that can't adapt will not survive. Their failure will be someone else's opportunity.

• The mobile revolution is giving birth to an entirely new economy, called the sharing economy.

• What guides the success of all mobile products—past, present, and future—is the Mobile Formula. It is based on human-first principles because mobile products are new extensions of ourselves. What we expect from them is what we wish for ourselves: an attractive body, having it all together emotionally, and getting smarter about the things that count. So, the Mobile Formula has three rules: the Body Rule, the Spirit Rule, and the Mind Rule.

- The Body Rule: the best mobile products are physically and functionally beautiful.

- The Spirit Rule: the best mobile products focus on what matters to us.

- The Mind Rule: the best mobile products learn as we use them.

Chapter 2

The Body Rule: The Best Mobile Products Operate by Beauty

Mind: **Learning**

Spirit: **Meaning**

Body: **Beauty**

TL;DR

- To be successful, mobile products must be beautiful. Beauty in mobile comes from efficiency and "wow."

- Efficiency: Nothing on mobile is wasted. Mobile designers make sure their products pass the thumb test.

- Wow: Beautiful mobile products trigger strong emotions. Mobile designers make sure their products pass the mom test.

- Mobile products need to work anywhere, so mobile designers need to carefully consider all the environments in which they'll be used. The products need to work like extensions of our bodies.

- Mobile designers rely on two types of design elements to build beautiful products: focusing and expanding.

- Case studies discussed in this chapter: Airbnb, Amazon Echo, Clara, Flipboard, Instagram, iPhone, KnockKnock, Pandora, Slack, and TrafficAlert.

Centuries ago, in medieval China, an emperor decided he wanted the most beautiful painting of a dragon ever made, so he commissioned it to be painted by a famed artist. The artist retired to a cave in a forest and started sketching.

Following months of intense effort, he returned to the emperor with his masterpiece.

The emperor looked at the painting. Disgusted by what he saw, he had the painter executed on the spot and the painting burned. What had the artist drawn?

Two parallel S-shaped curves, which seemingly could have been drawn by any calligrapher.

Years later, during a hunt, the emperor got lost in a forest. While resting, he noticed a cave and wandered in. On the walls were hundreds of dragon sketches. Realizing that this was the cave where the artist had gone, the emperor followed all the iterations, one by one—until he finally landed on the two simple curves.

The emperor realized the artist was right: the dragon had been perfectly captured by these two simple yet masterly lines. The lines were beauty.

The remorseful emperor named the forest after the artist.

⑈ ⑈ ⑈

I love this story. Beauty is so confounding! It baffles us.

Does beauty have a cheat sheet? Is there a surefire recipe to attain it that could help us avoid the emperor's mistake?

It's hard to argue with the fact that successful mobile products are beautiful. Picture the iPhone, Instagram, Airbnb, Flipboard. We can recognize beauty in these products and services, but no one can quite put their finger on it. Turns out, defining beauty has been a challenge for centuries.

To arrive at a definition of beauty that might help us create winning mobile products, let's look at how people define beauty in the arts. First, objectively: beauty is efficiency. Second, subjectively: beauty is wow. We will start with the objective definition.

Beauty and Efficiency: Nothing Is Wasted

The ancient world, particularly Ancient Greece, believed that beauty is quantifiable and objective. They discovered that everything in the universe could be explained by math.

Greek architects and sculptors devised the famous Golden Mean,[20] a perfect balance of symmetry, proportion, and harmony that could be expressed mathematically. Greek mathematician Pythagoras even applied this objective evaluation to music. He found that the relation between harmonious sounds is a simple numerical ratio, which became the basis for all music theory.

These objective definitions of beauty ruled the European art world for centuries. In the late eighteenth century, the French Royal Academy of Painting and Sculpture had a quasi-monopoly on taste. It organized art exhibitions, such as the Salon de Paris, showcasing what was deemed at the time the most beautiful artwork in the world.

But just when the French believed they had reached an objective definition of beauty, it escaped them when a group of artists, including painter Édouard Manet, whose work had been rejected by the Salon, started a movement—Impressionism—that would turn art on its head.

Impressionist artists purposefully covered their canvasses with hundreds of visible brushstrokes to emphasize light, texture, and movement in the composition. Traditionalists countered that the paintings were ugly, that they didn't look exactly like their original subjects. But Impressionism endured to become one of the most influential movements in the history of art.

Impressionism was a wake-up call for the art world, a reminder that beauty is polarizing. Some people will love a piece of art; others will hate it.

Remember the example of the Chinese dragon? The emperor didn't recognize how beautiful it was until he understood the artist's approach. Then he came to love it.

ılı· ılı· ılı·

Dragons and Impressionist paintings may not be for everyone in the twenty-first century, but mobile products are. They have to be. As we discussed, the mobile revolution is here to stay because billions of people already have a personal device of their own: their smartphone. And, as is the case with the iPhone, people pull it out on average 110 times a day.[21] We seemingly can't live without them.

So every mobile designer has an impossible mission: they have to delight billions of people 110 times a day with something they can only touch or talk to.

How do they do that? When it comes to mobile products, beauty appears through efficiency. This is often referred to as the Birkhoff formula[22]:

$$M = O/C$$

George David Birkhoff was a mathematician known for his work on differential equations. He published this mathematical theory of beauty in 1933 in his book *Aesthetic Measure,*[23] which is still used today by professionals who research, design, and assess products and services for their usability.

In the Birkhoff formula, M is a measure of beauty, O of simplicity, and C of complexity. What it says is that beauty (M) increases with simplicity (O) and decreases with complexity (C.)

In other words, similar to the principle behind the ancient Greeks' Golden Mean, beauty is creating order out of chaos. Let's look at a few examples.

From the very beginning, the best products of the mobile revolution have been gorgeous. They wow us. Remember the launch of the first iPhone? Steve Jobs on stage, giving the keynote address at the annual Apple user conference.[24] "I have been looking forward to this for two and a half years," he said. "Today, Apple is going to reinvent the phone."

"[It's] a magical product," he said as he gently slid the iPhone out of his pocket, a move he had rehearsed for hours to make sure it would be smooth. The beauty of the iPhone was right there, obvious to everyone in the room. The crowd gave Jobs a standing ovation.

But its enthusiastic reception was about more than the iPhone's physical attractiveness—it was about its sleek operation, its efficiency. "iPhone uses [our fingers] to create the most revolutionary interface since the mouse," Jobs added. There was no stylus, no external keyboard, no mouse. It epitomized the ultimate in simplicity for a tech product. The device was created to be easy to use by everyone.

As Jobs suggested, the lowest common denominator between all these people using their smartphones is their fingertips. So to create a satisfying user experience for everyone, designers rely on what's called the *thumb test*.

The thumb test is one of the most important rules for mobile design. To pass the thumb test, a task should be easily completed by a user with a thumb of average size and without incidentally hitting an unrelated link, button, or other design element by mistake.

One of the masters of this is Pandora, the personalized radio service.[25] Their team has created a whole radio station around the thumb. The service pulls from one of the world's largest and most sophisticated music libraries to build customized stations on the fly. It would be ugly to go through hundreds of thousands of albums to listen to a few good songs, don't you think? Even to find my favorite song, I would not have that much patience.

What Pandora did, though, was beautiful. It took the thumb test so seriously that it came up with a verb for it: *thumbing*. It creates personalized radio stations on the go based on a user's preferences. People can alter the program of their stations by thumbing a song up or down, which means liking or nixing it.

Pandora relies on what's called the Music Genome,[26] which is a set of 400 different attributes defining the musical qualities of a song, from melody to rhythm, syncopation to lyrics. Using that Music Genome, it broke the complexity of musical taste into a very simple decision—if you like a song, you hit the thumb-up button; if you dislike it, you hit thumb-down.

Thumb-ups are an objective sign of beauty.

A few years ago, another beautifully designed mobile product made headlines: Instagram. The mobile photo-sharing, video-sharing, and social networking service captures the minds of 400 million users.[27] Facebook purchased it in 2012 for $1 billion. At the time the steep acquisition price of Instagram was surprising, but several recent acquisitions have made the deal seem like a bargain.[28] For instance, Google bought Nest, the company that designs gorgeous smart thermostats, for $3 billion. These enormous numbers are telling: some Fortune 100 companies place a tremendous value on beauty.

Instagram is another example of an ambitious group of entrepreneurs who brought the beauty of efficiency to mobile. They turned the complex process of photo and video editing into a couple of clicks, essentially enabling anyone to create and share gorgeous photos and videos. It became a new kind of self-expression, a new way to relate with the world around us, a new outlet to create and share beautiful memories.

Just as the Chinese artist from our earlier story was able to simplify a dragon to its essence—two parallel S curves—Instagram compiled the entire process of developing negatives in a darkroom, printing photographs, and mailing prints to friends and family down to the essential: a couple of taps.

᭙ᬗ ᭙ᬗ ᭙ᬗ

A company I've had the chance to advise, GreenOwl Mobile, which gives drivers a safe and intuitive way to reach their destinations,[29] goes a step beyond the thumb test.

GreenOwl's service, TrafficAlert, is completely hands-free. It delivers audio alerts contextually, in response to real-time conditions, and relies on voice recognition to interact with users. It keeps drivers focused on where it matters: the road. When an accident or some other delay comes up ahead, it sends drivers alternative routes based on their current location, allowing them to adjust on the spot. As a result, it has become one of the leading traffic services in Canada and is quickly expanding internationally.

GreenOwl's beauty is that its operation doesn't even require a thumb.

In a similar vein, some mobile pioneers are creating smartphone apps that are completely invisible. Design guru and author Golden Krishna writes that "the best interface is no interface."[30] The process, he argues, is more important than the screen it is strapped in.

Take a service like Amazon Echo, the voice command device from Amazon, and its automated response persona, Alexa.[31] You don't need to fiddle with its smartphone app at all. All you need to do is talk to Alexa and ask, for instance, to listen to a song or the latest news. The product takes it from there.

Clara, which auto-magically schedules meetings when you forward her an e-mail, is another example of an invisible app.[32] Clara allows you to remain focused on what it is you're doing. You no longer need to pause, open your calendar, enter people's e-mail addresses, set up a dialing number, and so on. The interface doesn't get in the way of the job to be done. It just does it. It's invisible.

Pushed to its limit, beauty is so efficient that it becomes invisible.

From simple gestures to hands-free products and all the way to invisible apps, we've covered the objective definition of beauty on mobile. Everything works effortlessly. Nothing is wasted. Now let's look at beauty subjectively.

Beauty and Wow: A Visceral Experience

Whereas Greek mathematician Pythagoras argued that everything could be explained with numbers and formulas, Russian author Leo Tolstoy argued that art is entirely subjective. In his book *What Is Art?*,[33] he makes the case that beauty is in the eye of the beholder.

There is something about beauty that's whimsical, argues Tolstoy. Almost magical. Beautiful things create empathy. If a viewer finds a painting beautiful, it is beautiful. If a listener is touched by a symphony, it is a moving piece of music. The person experiencing a piece of art is the one to decide its artistic value, not the artist.

Beauty is the feeling created within us, the primal reaction. It resonates deep. When we encounter it, we get completely wowed.

In mobile, too, beauty comes through this wow factor. Let's consider some examples.

To understand what users want, Flipboard personalized news service[34] founder Mike McCue uses a clever approach: the mom test.[35]

He founded Flipboard in 2010 to transform the way people read and spread the news. Users can follow their favorite news sources from around the world and share stories, images, and videos that reflect their interests.

McCue tells his employees to think constantly about their mothers' reactions—real or imagined—to the things they're building.

"[Imagine] you're sitting down at Thanksgiving, and your mom asks, 'So, what are you doing? What are you building?' If you start to give an answer, and her eyes are glazing over, and she doesn't really understand what you're saying, you know you're off to a bad start."

McCue goes on to describe what the mom test truly entails: "Think about how the average person—the person who could benefit from technology, but who is not necessarily adept with technology—might react to a product. They need to get what the product is about and be able to use it. And, they need to want to use it."

McCue believes that seeing the world through the lens of a friend or family member is the key to building products that delight everyone.

And if you can build a product that delights everyone, you have passed the mom test. You have created wow.

॥॥· ॥॥· ॥॥·

Airbnb vacation rental service[36] founder Joe Gebbia goes a step beyond the mom test. He says that designing great mobile products requires a deep understanding of what people want.

The company was founded in 2007 by two roommates struggling to make ends meet in downtown San Francisco. They offered travelers an air mattress and home-cooked breakfast in their living room. Today, Airbnb has over 1.5 million listings in 190 countries.

"We put ourselves in the shoes of the person we're designing for," Gebbia writes on his blog.[37] "And I think that's a universal principle. Whether it's in the physical world or whether it's online, surprisingly enough, the principles are pretty much the same."

Take Airbnb's wish list feature. For a few years, registered Airbnb users were able to star the properties they browsed and save them to a list. Gebbia's team felt that a star was a generic symbol and decided to change it to a heart. A heart is much more aspirational than a star. It appeals to users' emotions, to their desire for adventure and unique experiences.

This simple change from a star to a heart resulted in a whopping 30 percent increase in the number of places on people's wish lists. They were wowed. As Gebbia put it, "[Changing this detail] showed the potential for something bigger."[38]

Hearting is a subjective sign of beauty.

⑊ ⑊ ⑊

KnockKnock, a mobile product from start-up Humin that helps you better manage your contacts,[39] applies a similar approach. "We get rid of the awkwardness of meeting people," says Humin cofounder Ankur Jain.

What I like about KnockKnock is that it feels very intuitive. The service mirrors the behavior of knocking on someone's door. The person on the other end gets to choose whether to open and, if so, what to share. It also uses Bluetooth to exchange contact information. There's no awkward typing.

Leading product design firm Frog Design[40] calls that approach *design thinking*, or human-centered design. Designers immerse themselves in the lives of their users, experiencing the constraints of their day-to-day lives, and consider every interaction as an opportunity to overcome these constraints. By doing so, they surprise and delight with real value. The products created with this approach tend to resonate more with their users because their conception is rooted in empathy. They feel universal.

Pushed to its limit, beauty resonates so deeply and collectively that it becomes universal.

Beauty in Context

Beauty doesn't exist in a vacuum. It takes into account the environment. The Chinese emperor was able to appreciate the beauty of the two S curves only when he saw them in context, in the cave amidst all the other versions of the dragon the artist had created.

This represents a particular challenge in mobile because there is no single environment where mobile products are used. By their very nature, they go wherever we go. They have to work well in any environment and with any other products they may encounter.

In fact, Silicon Valley design guru Joe Robinson recommends that designers read science fiction books[41] because it helps them picture what the future might look like. When designers understand their users' environment, they can create products that work contextually.

Take the example of that first iPhone. At the time of launch, Apple designers realized that there were three things people like to do on the go: listen to music, talk to friends, and browse the Internet. Until the iPhone, they needed three separate devices to do this: an iPod, a cell phone, and a PDA (personal digital assistant).

The iPhone was presented as three devices beautifully combined into one: an iPod with a wide screen, a phone with touch control, and a mini web browser. People no longer needed to carry three devices with them. All they needed was to have this one. The combination itself was beautiful because it was perfectly suited to the user's environment—being on the move.

Now let's look at a workplace environment and business messaging service Slack.[42] The service has been called the "fastest growing business app ever."[43] Slack's founder, Stewart Butterfield, who also founded the photo-sharing service Flickr,[44] is a designer with a deep background in cognitive science.

With Slack, Butterfield is revolutionizing workplace communication. In most companies, discussion is scattered. A team of engineers calls for a meeting: Was it by phone, or e-mail, or online chat? Keeping track of all these channels is hard. Slack integrates these communications systems into a central location, so tracking things and reaching colleagues becomes easier.

IT departments love Slack. Why? Butterfield made sure that Slack would be very easy to set up and maintain. It is beautiful because it plugs right into any work environment.

To understand why this is so meaningful, you have to keep in mind that companies rely on many tools to operate. These tools need to work well together. If one is poorly designed or breaks, it can have a domino effect and paralyze the whole business. So IT departments are rightfully concerned about any new technology, especially when it needs to interact with many other critical tools such as e-mail or chat.

Unfortunately for IT, mobile products started as personal devices. Unlike computers, which were first adopted by companies, smartphones emerged in the hands of people first. So, mobile was brought into the workplace by employees: the janitors, the salespeople, the administrative assistants, the financial analysts. Companies had to adapt to the popularity and utility of smartphone apps after the fact.

Before services like Slack, IT departments found it difficult to adopt mobile because they felt it was forced upon them. They didn't control which employees had what apps on their smartphones because the smartphones belonged to the employees.

Mobile services like Slack acknowledge this concern and are designed specifically to address it. They harness the beauty of efficiency and wow to function well in all business environments.

Now that we understand that beauty on mobile equals efficiency and wow, and that mobile beauty is attained when it works seamlessly in any environment, let's look under the hood. How do mobile designers take these concepts and use them in their designs?

Building for Beauty: Mobile Products As Extensions of Our Body

Because they build off of human-first principles, mobile products sometimes appear so simple that they feel obvious, as in anybody could make one, just like the dragon painting we discussed earlier.

Truth is, the most beautiful mobile products are the result of an enormous amount of work. Mobile designers rely on two types of carefully considered design elements to achieve this beauty: focusing and expanding. Focusing elements build trust by being predictable. Once trust is established, expanding elements allow the experience to be personalized to a user's moods and environment.

Focusing design elements can be an obvious call to action, like the "OK" button of a subscription form, but they also manifest as more subtle interactions that seamlessly immerse people in the world around them and deepen their relationship to it.

They are a necessary component of a solid relationship between a user and a mobile product. They build trust, respect, and familiarity over time. They make life easier for users by establishing simple and predictable rules of communication. Through them, mobile products add transactional value and with time, they become indispensable.

As trust builds, users start to expect more. This is where expanding design elements come in.

Expanding design elements look like simple requests for permission, such as to access a user's address book, track their location, or send them push notifications. They enable deep personalization to a user's mood, time, and place. Users get more value out of doing less because the product itself notifies them about ways they can use it to simplify their life when and where it matters.

〜 〜 〜

Even though it's relatively difficult to build a mobile product today, I believe that things will go the other way.

Think about the early days of automobiles. Initially, they were conceived in advanced workshops and assembled by an army of engineers, technicians, and plant workers. Now, components are manufactured all over the world and assembled in factories populated more by robotic machinery than people.

Computer manufacturers followed the same model. Initially, computers were designed and built top to bottom by a very savvy and cross-functional device team. Today, companies like Dell buy premade components and assemble computers on demand, as orders come in.

Mobile devices themselves are already a set of components beautifully put together. I believe this will happen in software too: smartphones apps will soon be a combination of standard components.

Reflect on this for a moment. Many smartphone apps need their users to sign up, so sign-up flows are likely to become a standard component. Already today, we're seeing the first attempts at standardizing sign-ups with Facebook Login.

Payment flow is also likely to become standard. Like any business, mobile companies need to make money, so most of them will need to accept payment. Tools offered by Stripe[45] are early attempts at providing a standard payment component for mobile.

These standard user flows will be the connecting tissue of smartphone apps. As they become standardized, they begin to resemble a utility, like the water and electricity in our homes. The details may vary at the tap or light switch, but the underlying systems are the same.

So it will be with mobile apps.

Building for Beauty: Focusing and Expanding Design Elements

Mobile designers rely on two types of design elements: focusing and expanding.[46]

Focusing design elements are the foundation of a solid relationship between a user and a mobile product. They provide easy access to the information a user is looking for. On the home screen of your smartphone, a focusing design element might be the red badge with a number at the top right corner of the app icon. It conveys that something new has happened since you last checked that screen. You missed something and need to get up to speed on what's going on with your friends. Time to reconnect!

Focusing design elements come in five types:

- **Onboarding,** such as tutorials, sign-up flows, help tips, and app store descriptions, convey to users the value they can get out of an app. Mobile companies have learned that there is a very short period of time and attention a user will grant them to make their case, so onboarding elements are critical. The best mobile apps use onboarding elements to deliver value to a user before they even sign up.

- **Single-task,** such as home screens, buttons, search bars, and predefined options, keep a user focused on what they need to accomplish. As mentioned, mobile companies often refer to the thumb test as one of the most important rules for mobile design. To pass the thumb test, a task should be easily completed by a user with a thumb of normal size and without incidentally hitting an unrelated link, button, or other design element by mistake.

- **Navigation,** such as side menus, navigation bars, and badges, allow users to transition between single tasks inside an app. Navigation is often hidden or positioned out of the way to allow single-task elements to take center stage. In most cases, a single navigation is best to keep things simple and easy to use. User reviews stating that an app is hard to use generally come from poorly designed navigation.

- **Performance,** such as crashes, slow-loading screens, broken links, timeouts, and other performance issues, tell users that an app is built on a broken foundation. When people discover they've invested time in a mobile product that doesn't work, they feel that their time is not being valued and they reject the product. This results in negative user reviews, disengagement, lost sales, and more. Performance focusing elements address these efficiency issues so they don't become problems.

- **Gestures,** such as tapping and swiping, are paradigms that exist only on the touch-enabled interface of mobile devices. Users expect predictability: one tap on an item expands it, a right swipe deletes it, etc. Imagine browsing for flights in a new travel app. You see a return ticket that fits your criteria and tap on it. What do you expect to happen? What if it doesn't? What if something else happens? How would you feel about using this app again?

Focusing design elements build trust, respect, and familiarity over time. As trust builds, users start to expect more. This requires access to personal information, which is where expanding design elements come in. They come in two types:

- **Pull,** such as alerts and pop-ups, prompt a user to grant permission to access personal data. This includes a user's contacts, photos, calendar, or even real-time location or health data. Getting permission from a user to pull this type of personal data allows an app to become contextual, to make an educated guess about what could be useful to a user at a specific time and place.

- **Push,** such as push notifications, are sent to a user's smartphone screen on behalf of an app. You've probably noticed them on your own phone—they pop up when you get a new e-mail, a friend makes an update on Facebook, or your crops are ready to harvest on Hay Day.[47] Push notifications keep a design so simple that users don't even need to launch the app anymore.

Well-engineered design gets out of the way because good mobile products enhance rather than obstruct a user's connection with the real world. Focusing design elements build trust by making it easy to do something that seems hard to do. Expanding design elements personalize people's experiences and deepen their connection to their environments. Mobile products that can do that become virtual extensions of their users' bodies.

Building Instagram for Beauty

Let's apply what we've learned to Instagram.

Yann (not his real name) is a senior at the University of Wisconsin majoring in marketing. He's a bright student with ambitious dreams, many friends, and a quirky sense of humor. But technology is not his strong suit. In fact, he'd much rather spend an evening hanging out with his friends than being behind a computer.

Yet, throughout the day he keeps pulling out his smartphone. He loves sharing his life on Instagram. Yann doesn't think about exposure, hues, or contrast when he immerses himself in Instagram.

"It's so easy and beautiful," he says as he scrolls through the feed of recent pictures posted by the people he follows. "My grandpa was a fashion photographer in the sixties. I love when he tells me stories about darkrooms and gelatin silver prints. It makes me feel like I'm in an episode of *Mad Men*. But I can't believe how much work taking pictures was."

What's behind Yann's passion for Instagram? How has this app been able to wow him? He loves the simplicity of the design because it lets him capture and share memories with his circle of family, friends, and online acquaintances. When he started using Instagram, he was instantly able to create a beautiful photo. All he needed to do was tap to select one of the gorgeous filters to tailor it to his mood of the moment, and then tap again to publish it. Immediately after posting it, he navigated to the feed and browsed through dozens of beautiful memories shared by others.

Recall the first time you saw an Instagram photo. Did it make you smile? Or maybe make you want to be there? Did you feel a connection to its author?

The simple taps required to create a picture are focusing design elements, gestures that make it easy to capture memories and share them. Similarly, the navigation bar at the bottom of the Instagram app is a focusing design element that allows you to switch from creating to browsing effortlessly.

Once he started to appreciate the experience of creating beautiful photos and videos, Yann felt comfortable allowing Instagram to share his content with his friends on Facebook and other social networks. By doing so, he put his reputation at risk, so he only did this once he trusted that the service wouldn't let him down, and that all his friends would enjoy it and find it fun.

Instagram used expanding design elements to request permission to access his address book only when Yann tried to share a photo with his friends for the first time. And it was clear from the language that Instagram would only use that information to share Yann's photos and videos. It wouldn't use it to share anything that Yann would not previously approve of.

As he built connections with other photographers whose pictures he liked, Yann started following them and gave Instagram permission to let him know via a push notification when these users posted more content.

By building trust through the simplicity and transparency of its design, Instagram earned the permission to connect Yann to a community of like-minded people. "I've made new friends. We have so much in common, I can't wait to meet them one day!"

For Yann, Instagram is now an extension of himself. It allows him to mesh with the world around him in new ways, and has made his relationships deeper and stronger.

Successful mobile products enhance people's lives like this. They replicate and amplify human behavior and interaction. Their natural beauty is inviting, their bare elegance makes room for the personalized content they bring to their users' attention, and their transparent flow removes obstacles to achieving what their users came to do.

Remember and Share

- All successful mobile products are beautiful, but how to define their beauty? Beauty in mobile comes from efficiency and wow.

- Efficiency: Greek mathematician Pythagoras believed that there is an objective definition of beauty, a formula like the Golden Mean. In mobile, it translates into elegance and simplicity. Nothing is wasted. Mobile designers use the thumb test to assess whether the product they're building passes this objective definition of beauty.

- Wow: Russian writer Leo Tolstoy argued that beauty is subjective. Beautiful art creates empathy. The visceral feeling we get is universal. In mobile, it translates into intuitive and human-centered approaches. Mobile designers use the mom test to assess whether the product they're building passes this subjective definition of beauty.

- But beauty doesn't exist in a vacuum. Mobile products that do not take context into account fail. Mobile designers carefully consider applicability to all sorts of environments when they design products.

- Mobile designers rely on two types of design elements to build beautiful products: focusing and expanding. Focusing elements build trust by being

predictable. Once trust is established, expanding elements allow the experience to be personalized to a
user's moods and environment. Today, it's still hard to
build beautiful mobile products. However, standards
will emerge that will make it easier.

Chapter 3

The Spirit Rule: The Best Mobile Products Give Us Meaning

Mind: **Learning**

Spirit: **Meaning**

Body: **Beauty**

TL;DR

- Mobile products are the ultimate personal products. They are with us always and understand what matters to us. Meaning from mobile comes through personalization and community.

- Personalization: Mobile products make us feel taken care of. They personalize everything to our mood and context.

- Community: Mobile products establish social norms and rituals that make us feel like we belong.

- Mobile products are companions that need to be aware of our context—what's happening outside and how we feel inside. They work like an extension of our spirit.

- Mobile companies use two types of filters to build products for meaning: internal and external.

- Case studies discussed in this chapter: Facebook, Google Glass, Siri, Tinder, Trulia, and Yelp.

Theo, a depressed writer living alone in Los Angeles, is going through a painful divorce. [48] As a way of coping with his feelings of isolation, he buys an *AI assistant*, similar to the iPhone's talking app, Siri. The artificial assistant's name: Samantha.

Samantha is an electronic device unlike any other. She's sophisticated, adaptable, and continuously supportive. Samantha makes Theo feel special. Although she's just a piece of software, Theo eventually falls in love with her.

Theo and Samantha are, of course, the main characters in Spike Jonze's Academy Award–winning movie, *Her*, which is a Hollywood version of what the mobile revolution can bring about.

Samantha is Theo's virtual soul mate. That at least is how he sees her. Everything he asks from her he gets. Samantha is thoroughly personalized to suit him. She's his perfect match.

But when he confesses to his friends that he and Samantha are *dating*, he is confronted with ridicule and judgment. Soon, Samantha also reveals that Theo is not her only relationship. In fact, she's promiscuous. Samantha is dating thousands of people. She's also spending time with other AI assistants, whose presence she prefers to humans. Theo is shattered.

Now, you might find the dynamic at play in *Her* a bit creepy. I wouldn't argue with that. But there's an important lesson inside of the fantasy: Great mobile products are a lot like Samantha. They're like an extension of our spirit.

One of the most disruptive aspects of mobile products is that they are the ultimate personal products. They are with us always. They know exactly what is meaningful to us. They personalize everything to our mood and context. They build trust and comfort—ingredients that naturally build attachment. We form emotional relationships with them.

On the flip side, relationships often get challenged when confronted with other people, our communities, and the world around us. Social norms and ritual apply.

What Samantha failed to grasp with Theo, successful mobile products need to understand: we are as much who we are *inside*, as individuals with unique feelings and emotions, as who we are *outside*, in our communities with their rules and compromises. And, we seek meaning from both inside and outside. Together, our inner and outer selves reflect the complete essence of our spirit.

To understand how our mobile products help us focus on the things that matter, let's first look inside: meaning is personalization. Then we'll look outside: meaning is community.

Meaning and Personalization: Feeling Cared For

We are all wired with anxieties that get triggered when we least expect them. In fact, psychology professor Roy Baumeister explains that it takes a lot of energy to keep this stress under control. He calls that energy *willpower*,[49] which is also the title of his best-selling book.

"Some people imagine that willpower is something you only use once in a while, such as when you are tempted to do something wrong. The opposite is true," he says. "Most people use their willpower many times a day, all day."

It all adds up to depletion of energy. That's when we most feel that we lose control.

"Depletion seems to be like turning up the volume on your life as a whole," Baumeister says.

Good mobile products turn the volume *down* on our life, and they do it by knowing a lot about us. The more they know about us, the more personalized they get. The more personalized they get, the better able they are to cater to our individual wants and needs.

A few months ago, my friend Jennifer (not her real name) started using dating service Tinder.[50] What does she enjoy about it most? It's highly personalized. Unlike more established dating services, Tinder only exists on smartphones and doesn't rely on impersonal algorithms to evaluate romantic potential between people.

Instead, it shows her people who are close to her geographically or socially, using her location and Facebook friends and interests to make her experience unique. It uses the smartphone's GPS to show only matches located nearby. And Jennifer also appreciates that the service uses Facebook Connect to create member profiles. Photos feel more authentic, and mutual friends are featured. It feels welcoming and safe.

"The first time I swiped," she says, "the screen of my phone was [immediately] inundated with an ever updating stream of male suitors: loafer-wearing Kip, 28, popping champagne on the deck of a boat (pretentious—swipe left!); shirtless Aaron, 31, winking at his reflection (bathroom-mirror selfie—swipe left!); tall, dimpled Peter, 30, smiling from a mountaintop (swipe right!)." Soon after, Peter liked her too. "I was hooked."

As well, she isn't assaulted by dozens of suitors, sending the same feeble introductory e-mail to every girl. Tinder's double-opt-in mechanism lets Jennifer interact with only those suitors she chooses. If you swipe right and they do too, it's a match and the pair can exchange private messages in the app.

Jennifer is one of over 50 million singles who participate in the cultural phenomenon that Tinder has become in less than four years. The service is available in 30 languages and claims over six billion matches since its launch in 2012. Some will use it in their hometown, others to spice up a business trip.

By being constantly connected to our environment, our mobile products alleviate decision fatigue. They sort through the millions of information bits we are bombarded with to show us only the ones that matter right here, right now. We give them permission to make these decisions on our behalf because they know enough about us to personalize everything.

This personalization is essential to what makes mobile products successful.-It puts *us* in complete control of the experience.

Sometimes, the experience we get from mobile is so personalized that we wouldn't be able to reproduce it otherwise. Life suddenly gets easier, because we are no longer hampered by circumstances beyond our control. Our stress level goes down, as in this example.

Not too long ago, I had an important meeting with a major partner, and as I was leaving my apartment it started raining. I decided to hail a cab.

Of course, there was no cab in sight. It took me a while to finally find one and by then, I was soaked and already late for my meeting. On top of this, when it came time to pay the fare, I didn't have enough cash so we had to stop by an ATM.

All I could think about was that I was going to lose my client. I blamed myself for not planning enough. I was upset at the rain for messing up the traffic. But really, I was afraid of losing a significant source of income. All because I couldn't find a cab.

Now that I started using Lyft and Uber, I no longer get stressed when I need a ride. All I need to do is pull up the service on my phone when I'm getting ready to go somewhere, get in the car when I'm notified that it's here to pick me up, and get out when I've arrived. It optimizes my itinerary in real time by routing around delays that before would have left me stuck in traffic. It even tells me ahead of time how much the fare will be. I no longer even need to "pay" in the traditional sense, because the fare is automatically charged to my credit card. I feel cared for, even pampered, because the service eliminates all the previous hassle of getting from point A to point B. It feels good.

Feeling taken care of in ways we cannot provide to ourselves is a reflection of what is important to us, of what has inner meaning to us. A bond naturally develops from this extreme personalization, similar to any relationship. This connection lifts our spirit, not unlike intense feelings such as love. And what gives us more meaning than being in love?

The meaning we create inside ourselves is what makes us unique. Outside, it's all about compromises. It's about how we live well in our communities. The best mobile products recognize this duality. We've looked inside, now let's look outside.

Meaning and Community: Social Norms and Rituals

In any relationship, our bonds are most tested when we go out among other people in the world. Social dynamics can be affected, as we saw earlier with Theo and Samantha. And because mobile is still new in our lives, we have not yet established norms and rituals for it.

Consider the question on many people's minds these days: Are we becoming too connected to our mobile devices? Some people (including myself at times) struggle to ever disconnect. We are always on our devices. Because every action on mobile is immediately recorded and broadcast, we compulsively obsess over every signal we get or don't get. It's been two hours already and no one commented on my post. Did I say something wrong? Why are people not paying attention? Maybe they don't like me anymore? Maybe they never did?

"Some people need to get unhooked," says best-selling author of *Hooked*, Nir Eyal, who wrote the foreword to this book.[51] He's certainly talking about the Theos of the world, who completely isolate themselves from others as their connection with their devices deepens. But what about the rest of us?

It's almost become cliché to hear complaints about everyone having their faces glued to their screens, stifling meaningful person-to-person communication. But do our smartphones disengage us from those around us, or connect us with them?

Some argue that people who suddenly shut down from a group and pull out their smartphone are detrimental to communities. But most of the time, I see people do this because they want to move the conversation forward, to be helpful. They want to fact-check something, or share a funny video. I don't think there's anything wrong with that.

In fact, research shows that mobile products create *deeper* bonds between users and their communities.

A study by the University of Florida, for instance, illustrates how mobile products make people feel more connected to those around them.[52] In 2013, a group of 339 undergraduates volunteered to answer questions about their smartphone activity. The researchers were interested in the frequency with which these students used their smartphones and what they were doing on them.

They found that participants spent two to three hours every day using their smartphone, of which about one hour was spent on social activities, including the use of social networks.

More importantly, the students were asked to answer questions about their social capital, which is the complex web of relationships that helps us live and work in our community. The results show that heavy smartphone users who use their mobile devices to connect with others and the world around them have stronger social capital. For example, these students were more involved in their local community, had more trusted people they could turn to for advice about making important decisions, and knew a greater number of people who could give them access to resources like professional publications.

With the mobile revolution, there is a lot more data about everything and everyone than ever before. And there is no going back. This abundance of information is mostly helpful, though sometimes it can expose our private lives—that inside world we've created through hyper-personalization of our mobile products—to a level of scrutiny that challenges our comfort level.

When we engage in mobile communities that operate by sharing intimate information about each other, we are in a sense observing each other—all the time. Research confirms that we tend to be on our best behavior when we know we are being observed.[53] But this unprecedented level of personal exposure that the mobile revolution demands in order to function is relatively uncharted territory.

Besides having such a vast amount of our personal information available to others, I have another concern: mobile companies have become, in fact, less business, more utility. They cannot go out of business because, just like our electricity and water, we expect our data to be around all the time.

Tech visionary and best-selling author of *You Are Not a Gadget,* Jaron Lanier, makes the case that companies that own massive amounts of data about us are effectively a public service. They should be nationalized, he argues, and their focus should shift from making a profit to protecting people.

But even government-run agencies need checks and balances. When government has had easy access to our personal information in the past, it has had nefarious consequences: surveillance states, "enemies" lists, persecution of dissidents. In places like China, it is still a reality today.

How do we protect ourselves from government overreach into our digital—and, therefore, personal—lives? We need to have the debate.

The same goes for commercial control of our personal data. The European debate around the "right to be forgotten" is an example of democracy in action, of people demanding more control of their digital selves.

So privacy loss is one of the biggest concerns when it comes to living in a mobile community. It's a topic that divides generations. Most millennials don't believe there is such a thing as privacy; many baby boomers feel that it's a right. This isn't saying that the former are naïve or the latter suspicious. This is saying that, in our own ways, we all want to feel in control. We want our mobile products to protect us, our loved ones, and our communities.

The disappointing launch of Google Glass is an example of what can happen when a mobile product fails to do so. It followed a typical losing playbook: inflated expectations, overpriced gadget ahead of its time, safety concerns, unclear use case, and lack of real-world testing. But none of those issues were its fatal flaw.

It didn't help that the initial launch was poorly handled. Right out of the gate, the press trashed the technical shortcomings: the battery didn't last, there were many crashes and bugs. One journalist even called it "the worst product of all time." But soft-launching a product before it is ready for prime time in order to use the feedback to improve is not uncommon in Silicon Valley.

What doomed Google Glass is that its power was seen as scary and out of the hands of its users. People felt it was built primarily to serve Google's own interests, that it was designed to collect data for the benefit of the tech giant rather than to serve the needs of its users. When exactly was it recording? Was it really turned off when it said it was? It triggered the same fear Theo experienced in *Her*, when Samantha revealed to him that she wasn't his exclusive AI assistant. Was she sharing his secrets with others? Theo felt betrayed and out of control because Samantha wasn't up front with him.

It extended into communities. People wearing Google Glass were asked to leave bars, movie theaters, and casinos. Privacy concerns were raised. Eventually, the product was removed from the market at the beginning of 2015.

Google is now trying to reinvent Google Glass as a hands-free display that could, for instance, be used by surgeons as they operate on a patient. I think it could be very valuable in these types of controlled situations.

The failed launch of Google Glass shows that we care about privacy rules in our mobile products—they have meaning to us—and we notice and react negatively when they are not clear.

Meaning in Context

Things only make sense in context. Samantha was able to focus on what mattered to Theo only once she understood what it was that had meaning to him. This is a particularly difficult challenge for mobile products because there are so many signals coming through at any point in time, from both inside and outside.

Take Apple's personal assistant, Siri. The reason it isn't used to its full potential today is that many of its recommendations are not pertinent.[54] It very often fails to contextualize and correctly interpret all the external information that's relevant to a user's request.

Siri was initially created to be a *do engine* that fulfills wishes. Unlike a search engine, which finds information but then leaves it up to you to take action, Siri was meant to do things for you, like buy movie tickets, place a confirmation call on your behalf, or reserve a table under your name.

But when it initially launched, it was far from being able to do all the things its creators wished it could do. Like many technologies, Siri's genesis goes back to military research. The original company was founded in the early days of the mobile revolution by three members of the CALO project, the largest AI project in history.[55] (CALO is an acronym for "Cognitive Assistant that Learns and Organizes.") The goal was to build a virtual assistant that would help military commanders. It used a complex technology called *natural language processing* to interpret what we say and turn it into commands a computer can understand.

Siri's secret sauce was to use natural language processing in a very sophisticated way. Instead of trying to guess what people say in a vacuum, which is a challenge for AI because there are so many variables and possibilities, Siri set out to understand sentences in context, using a smartphone's GPS, address book, calendar, and more to interpret meaning.

Early on, Siri missed the point too often. Its responses to questions and requests weren't contextual or even relevant.

As such, Siri never lived up to its hype. People see it mostly as an intriguing gadget with some amusing uses, or as a hands-free tool when they are driving or otherwise unable to use the keyboard. Some use it to manage their calendar, for example, when they need to schedule an alarm, set a reminder, or cancel a meeting. And that's about it.

In *Her,* Samantha was a more evolved version of Siri—it was what Siri wanted to be. But that was a movie, and mobile products must function in reality. And the reality is that mobile products can help us focus on what matters only if they understand the context we're in.

With Siri, we've looked at external context. Now let's use Facebook to examine how our internal context is just as important.

Many people who wished to file a complaint on Facebook used to give up halfway. Someone would start reporting, say, a photo someone else had posted and then would change their mind at the last minute and abandon the process.

The Facebook team discovered that the reason people would not go through with reporting pictures or posts they initially found offensive was that they were afraid it would upset the person who posted it. That person was their friend most of the time, and they didn't want to hurt them. They were placing their friend's feelings above their own.

To solve the problem, Facebook called on a group of experts in behavioral economics. "[Unlike traditional economics,] behavioral economics does not assume that people are rational," says Dan Ariely, best-selling author of *Predictably Irrational*[56] and professor of behavioral economics at Duke University. Much of Ariely's research revolves around how people make choices and the resulting effect on incentives.

The complaint form had been designed to be as neutral as possible. When people reported a photo, it asked them to select the reason they were reporting it: it's insulting, or it's blurry, or it tags me but I'm not actually in it, and so on. It appealed to people's common sense and rational brain.

But reason is often misinterpreted as judgment. The tone of the abuse report form felt judgmental to users. Even though it asked to report a judgment on the picture, people were afraid it would be interpreted as a judgment on the person. Such a complaint could put the entire friendship at risk.

The behavioral experts suggested an alternative approach. Instead of listing neutral reasons for submitting a complaint about what the *poster* had done, why not offer a choice of what the *user* was feeling at the time they decided to file a report. Were they feeling insulted by the content? Were they concerned that the photo they got tagged in didn't make them look good? Were they upset because their political views had been exposed?

The abuse report became a way for users to share how they felt about something that was bothering them, without incriminating, judging, or accusing their friends. They were able to express negative feelings without compromising their relationship.

The completion rate of the complaint form went from single digit to almost 100 percent.

Facebook didn't invent a new type of communication. In fact, many family therapists use this technique when they help couples improve their relationship. Facebook simply recognized that people think about and value their place within communities. It is another reflection of their inner selves, their spirit.

This deep understanding of our internal and external lives is powered under the hood by a gigantic personalization machine. This machine can be so effective that people become emotionally attached to their mobile products. We come to rely on them extensively because they know what's meaningful to us as individuals. It's an extraordinary relationship, when you think about it. Let's look at the mechanics of how it is achieved.

Building for Meaning:
Mobile Products as Extensions of Our Spirit

Because mobile products are always with us, they know exactly what is meaningful to us as individuals and as members of our communities. Mobile companies rely on two types of filters—internal and external—to satisfy the needs of both relationships. Internal filters enable personalization by learning about us, who we care about, and where we go. Once they understand what matters to us personally, external filters allow the experience to be shared and enjoyed with other people.

Internal filters can be as simple as our current location or our address book, but they also enable more subtle location-based services that effectively connect people to their environment without them being involved.

Take real estate marketplace Trulia, for instance. Most people looking for an apartment or home prefer to search on the go, while they're actually in their favorite neighborhood, rather than from behind a computer screen. Trulia completely eliminates the tedious research part of the process.

Once Trulia knows a user's criteria for a home, it sends them personalized push notifications whenever a suitable listing is available nearby. It even contacts property managers on their behalf and helps them be first in line to check desirable properties. Users no longer need to browse themselves; Trulia does it for them. It's like a real-life version of Samantha, who personalized everything for Theo without even having to consult with him.

We first tested this concierge feature during my time at Trulia and were concerned that people might not like it. After all, we were making big decisions on their behalf and acting as an automated rental agent. We thought many people would complain, so we made it very easy for them to opt out.

On the contrary, user satisfaction went up. The process of looking for a place to purchase or rent is so stressful that anything that made it easier was welcome.

As our mobile products come to understand what matters to us, we expect them to meet more than our individual needs. They also need to help us integrate in our communities. This is where external filters come in. Done right, external filters power healthy communities where everyone feels respected.

External filters can take the form of a privacy policy, which governs what a product can and cannot reveal about its users, or compliancy rules, which dictate what can and cannot be said or done about members of a community, or a double opt-in mechanism, which regulates how people meet others. They establish social norms and rituals for our mobile products.

Users feel that they belong in a community because the product itself helps them respect others' needs and act in ways that the group will accept. This makes them feel like they matter because they are part of something bigger than themselves.

To be effective, external filters need to be very transparent, otherwise users feel manipulated, even betrayed. Recall how our friend Theo in *Her* felt when he no longer was certain what information Samantha was sharing with others. The policy itself matters less than how clearly it is communicated, as we saw in the real-life counterexample of Google Glass.

Building for Meaning: Internal and External Filters

Mobile companies use two types of filters to sort through the barrage of signals we constantly receive from our environment and create meaning out of it. Internal filters personalize our experience based on our mood, context, and preferences.[57]

Internal filters come in two forms:

- **Place,** such as current location, home or work address, and other points of interest, power the what's called *location-based services.* Place filters keep us connected to our environment in ways we couldn't be without them. Mobile companies that power these services have transformed our lives profoundly. People no longer need to decipher maps to go places or rely on local insiders for cool restaurants.

- **People,** such as address books and social plug-ins, make it easy for us to connect with our friends and loved ones and reach exactly whom we need when we need them. They make sure we have control over who sees what when. They protect us and our social circles. Mobile companies use people filters to let us share photos and videos with selected groups, or suggest that we send our friends a nice message on their birthday, or create custom groups to, for example, invite friends to a holiday bash or message our book club.

Because they are so personal, internal filters build an emotional connection between users and their mobile products. Just as with friends and loved ones, building a relationship needs to survive the test of being out in the world. This is where external filters come in. To be effective, they need to be very transparent.

There are three types of external filters:

- **Policy,** such as privacy rules, terms and conditions, and other legalese, govern how users' information can and should be used. These filters protect members of a community from threats like government monitoring and nuisances like unsolicited advertising. Mobile companies are often forced by law to implement and enforce policy filters.

- **Popularity,** such as reviews and ratings, establish and protect users' reputations. They facilitate the informal vetting process we go through as we become accepted by a group or community. They express the respect others have for our skills, tastes, values, and opinions. They are often used by mobile companies to ensure that members of a community play by the rules.

- **Permission,** such as opt-in/opt-out features and abuse reports, regulate how others can impact us. They are especially important because many of us never disconnect from our mobile products. Permission filters ensure that we can decide what others can and can't do with our personal data, and set the boundaries for how they can communicate with us. Mobile companies must be very mindful of not taking users for granted.

Mobile products are the ultimate personal products. They cater to our every need. Internal filters personalize everything to make us feel understood and taken care of as an individual. External filters create the social norms we need to feel like we belong to the communities we care about. This is how mobile products become extensions of their users' spirit.

Building Facebook and Yelp for Meaning

Let's look at how Facebook uses internal filters to personalize the experience of the most adept users.

Seasoned Facebook users tend to have more friends than average and as a result, there is a lot of content for them to browse, from profiles to pictures, posts, pages, and more. Most of the time, they will rely on the News Feed feature to give them a snapshot of what's most relevant right here, right now.

When I worked at Facebook, I sat a few desks away from the team that was in control of the settings and parameters of the News Feed. One of its charges was to develop internal filters to better personalize the experience of Facebook users.

It is hard to imagine a more complex task than making sense of thousands of rankings and preferences in real time. But instead of monopolizing control of the process, the News Feed team made the deliberate choice to give users direct access to internal filters so that *they* could control the content of their own News Feed.

The Facebook team realized that advanced users wanted more than just better controls and settings, or a fancier News Feed. They wanted their voices heard. This is why internally they are called *content producers*, in contrast with less sophisticated users who consume content instead of producing it.

An average user may not notice this, but experienced users craft their Facebook posts to make sure they reach exactly whom they're intended for. They often create multiple groups of friends based on shared interests or locations. They even have the ability to give those groups names: "amateur chess club," or "Sally's birthday bash," or "San Francisco hikers."

Facebook doesn't try to get the content producers to do anything new. It simply makes it easy for them to share the things that matter to them with their community.

᯽ ᯽ ᯽

Now let's look at how crowdsourced reviews service Yelp uses external filters to build community.

Clay (not his real name) is a 53-year-old general contractor in Concord, California. He started his business more than 30 years ago and almost had to close it down during the last recession. Things suddenly picked up in 2011, when one of his customers asked if they could leave him a review on Yelp. Clay and his small crew had done a great job with their bathroom remodel.

Founded in 2004 by former PayPal employees Russel Simmons and Jeremy Stoppelman, Yelp[58] publishes local business reviews through crowdsourcing. Over the past few years, I've been lucky to count them as one of my partner companies.

At the time, Clay wasn't familiar with Yelp. He downloaded the app on his smartphone and created an entry for his business. Soon, other happy customers left him reviews. It felt really good to see the quality of his work acknowledged publicly. Yelp reviews and ratings are examples of popularity external filters that, such as in Clay's case, make users feel valued and appreciated.

Within a few months, Clay noticed that he was receiving significantly more requests for quotes. Until then, new business had come through referrals (and there was never quite enough of them), but these seemed to be coming out of the blue. People would reach out and mention the great Yelp reviews.

Clay used to work with the same trusted specialists on his jobs, an electrician and a plumber, who over time had become his friends. He had been concerned that they might want to retire soon without finding the time to groom the next generation. When contracts started to increase, his business reached the capacity it needed to support a larger crew with younger members he could train himself.

Today, Clay's business has more than doubled. He is not alone—Yelp has millions of reviews and has become a rainmaker for small businesses. A 2011 study published by Harvard Business School[59] revealed that for every star in a review, the sales for the business being reviewed is affected by 5 to 9 percent.

I asked Clay what he worries about most and his answer didn't surprise me: the competition. But I failed to grasp his real meaning. Clay has more business than he needs, so he's not concerned about losing bids to his competitors. Instead, he's scared that one of them will leave him a fake negative review on Yelp.

Fake reviews, as you can imagine, are a common practice. To filter them out, Yelp has developed a proprietary tool that marks as many as one in four reviews as suspicious. Although Yelp has had to deal with lawsuits about review accuracy, the company's filtering algorithm is one of the industry's most effective. Because of that, Yelp has gained the trust of 85 million people[60] who use its mobile app every month to find a nearby restaurant for lunch, a late-night bar to end a fun date, or a contractor like Clay for a home remodel.

External filters, such as popularity filters, can make or break a business. The judgments people make about us carry a lot of weight, and we have little control over it.

Remember and Share

- One of the most disruptive aspects of mobile products is that they are with us always. They understand what matters to us both from inside, as individuals with unique feelings and emotions, and from outside, as members of communities with social rules and rituals. Meaning from mobile comes through personalization and community.

- Personalization: The more mobile products know about us, the more personalized they get. So people come to rely on them extensively and often become emotionally attached to them.

- Community: As our bond grows inside, so does the need for privacy and other social norms outside. We need big business and government to protect our personal data and treat it with respect.

- To help us focus on the things that matter, mobile products need to be aware of our context, both what's going on outside and how we feel inside.

- Mobile companies use two types of filter to build for meaning: internal and external. Internal filters enable personalization by learning about us, who we care about, and where we go. Once they understand what matters to us personally, external filters allow the experience to be shared and enjoyed with other people.

Chapter 4

The Mind Rule: The Best Mobile Products Learn as We Use Them

Mind: **Learning**

Spirit: **Meaning**

Body: **Beauty**

TL;DR

- To be successful, mobile products must adapt constantly. They do it fast, and slow.

- Fast: Mobile companies relentlessly learn from their users and adapt to their rapidly evolving needs. Adapting is a matter of survival.

- Slow: Mobile companies must reinvent themselves as they break new ground. They have no choice.

- By constantly analyzing and optimizing information, mobile products work like an extension of our mind.

- Mobile companies use two types of tools to learn from their users and get better at what they do: scientific and artistic.

- Case studies discussed in this chapter: Facebook, Lyft, Nokia, WhatsApp, Viber, and Yelp.

On my first day working at Facebook, I got a booklet titled, "Facebook was not originally created to be a company."

That sounded almost like a question. What, then, was it created to be? The answer was on the overleaf: "It was built to accomplish a social mission—to make the world more open and connected."

Great mobile companies start with big visions. Not technology visions. Visions for a better world. Human-first visions. They assemble and organize amazing teams. The products they build often look like dreams come true. Overnight successes.

But where does greatness in mobile come from? How is it born?

Think of Uber. Or WhatsApp. Would you say you understand why or how they became so essential to so many people? Do you feel you were *warned* that they would matter one day? Do you think of them as the result of a lot of trial and error?

Personally, I couldn't figure out the secret sauce. I understood that these companies had all the pieces in place. They were in the right place at the right time. They had supersmart people backing them. They worked really hard. And then . . . what? Magic happened? They got lucky? How did they do this? Why them and not another start-up?

I ask myself the same questions about anyone who achieves something greater than themselves. How did they do it? How do people actually go about achieving what most people think is completely impossible?

According to *New York Times* best-selling author Robert Greene, top achievers apply a skill called *mastery* to everything they do.

In his book *Mastery*, Greene says that mastery starts with what he calls apprenticeship. "We love the myth of the artist as creator," he says.[61] But the truth is a lot less glamorous: all great masters relentlessly practice their craft for thousands and thousands of hours. They learn and persist until an opportunity to break through comes along. Then, they become masters.

Take Nelson Mandela, someone who always fascinated me (and many others). The son of a prominent political figure in South Africa, he became a political activist in opposition to the racial segregation laws in place in South Africa at the time, called apartheid.[62]

Continually evaluating the political landscape, Mandela learned quickly and constantly adapted his tactics against apartheid in the face of changing conditions. Initially an advocate of nonviolent action, he became the commander of a revolutionary army, which led to a sentence of life imprisonment. Prison didn't stop him. He befriended his jailers, becoming a potent symbol of grace under adversity. People around him praised his character. He refused to compromise with the racist regime in place. His fame only grew bigger.

In 1990, Mandela was freed from prison. The next year, the last remaining apartheid laws were repealed. In 1994, Mandela became the first black president of South Africa.

By overseeing the peaceful transition of his country from apartheid—an unjust system that had been in place since 1948—in only four years, Nelson Mandela became a symbol of freedom and hope. To some, it may seem like it happened overnight. Instead, it took a lifetime.

Along the way, Mandela reinvented himself many times: from an activist to an outlaw, then to a convict, a hero, a head of state. Ultimately, he received a Nobel Peace Prize for his life's work. This came as a by-product of achieving mastery.

Mobile products obviously are not on the same level as Mandela's struggle against apartheid, but they operate by the same playbook. They are always learning with and from their users, by breaking down problems into smaller, more manageable steps that can be solved relatively quickly. They operate like our mind, which constantly analyzes and optimizes what it perceives.

When they find something that works, they do more of it. Gradually, each problem they solve brings them closer to becoming masters at their craft. This is when we notice them. Their seemingly overnight success is a by-product of aiming for mastery.

We'll begin by looking at how mobile companies learn fast, by tirelessly solving problems and seeking impact. Then, we'll examine how they learn slow, by reinventing themselves and breaking new ground.

Learning Fast: Relentlessly Adapting to Us

Remember when I told you in the previous chapter how I started using Lyft and Uber when I needed to go places? I'm not the only one by far.

Early on, car service company Lyft was facing a challenge every business would love to have: too much demand.

On Friday night in particular, rides are in short supply because many more people need them. Plus, even though they make more money on Friday night, Lyft drivers often take the evening off to have a social life of their own.

For passengers, this dearth of drivers could create the same type of stress I experienced when I couldn't find a cab, and Lyft learned early on that it needed to find a solution and increase the supply of available rides.

To solve the problem, the company reached out to a team of behavioral economists.[63] Recall from the previous chapter that behavioral economists believe most people do not make decisions based solely on reason.

The researchers sat down with a dozen Lyft drivers, trying to understand how they decided when to work and when not to work. They found out that Wednesday morning is the time when drivers make weekend plans, so this is when they made the decision to work on Friday night or take it off.

Based on that insight, the researchers recommended that every Wednesday morning, Lyft should show drivers the opportunity cost of taking Friday night off.

Then they tested and compared different ways to communicate this to the drivers. They learned that drivers were more willing to work on a Friday night after they understood not how much they would make if they did but how much they would lose if they didn't.

You may be thinking that this feels manipulative. If you do, I understand. However, Lyft's intent is to meet the demand of its customers and maximize the profit of its drivers. Because of its iterative approach, it optimized its offering until it was able to give drivers enough reasons to meet the demand of its customers on Friday night.

What I find particularly impressive is how Lyft was able to balance and optimize supply and demand in real time and adapt to the needs of both drivers and passengers.

For mobile companies, learning fast like this isn't optional; it's a matter of survival. On mobile, user behavior changes at an accelerated pace, as does the technology that caters to it. Every few weeks, people become more proficient with their mobile products. Every 18 to 24 months, they upgrade to a new one.

There is no slowing down. Mobile companies know that they cannot move at a leisurely pace. What worked a month ago no longer works today. What was enough in a given context no longer is in a different environment. What seemed worth selling is suddenly offered for free from a competitor.

They need to learn and get better fast. Whether they're at the early stages of building and launching a product, in the customer acquisition phase, or in a more mature phase of monetization, they still need to relentlessly adapt.

Take mobile messaging giant WhatsApp.[64] It is constantly adding new features—groups, videos, emojis. People love these, so they use WhatsApp all the time. The more they use it, the more WhatsApp learns what they like and the better it gets. The better it gets, the more people use it.

The WhatsApp team solves one small problem after the other, as quickly as possible. It goes through a relentless trial-and-error process to mirror customers' needs and provide those things people want in the real world—assurances that their message was read, that the person they are trying to contact is checking in, and so on. In developing countries like India, where they often still pay for text messages and data usage, people love WhatsApp because it lets them send messages to their friends for free.

Because it creates a product that keeps getting better over time, it gets more and more people to use it. As of June 2015, it had an astonishing 800 million users.[65]

Learning Slow: Breaking New Ground

People who accomplish great things learn fast . . . and by doing so, they improve incrementally until they slowly reinvent themselves and achieve a level of mastery.

Soon after he took his company public, Trulia cofounder Sami Inkinen set out to reinvent himself completely.[66] He became a triathlon world champion. In 2014, he and his wife broke the world record for rowing unassisted from San Francisco to Hawaii. Inkinen jokingly says that his biggest accomplishment is that after such an intense experience, he is still married.

I asked him what his secret was for accomplishing these impossible goals. "If you can measure something, you can improve it," he said. "Every time I try something new, I write down three things I could improve doing next time."

Successful mobile companies do the same. As they find ways to keep up with the pace of innovation and learn from their users, they strive to break new ground. They target new users or launch new offerings. Each time, they need to learn everything from scratch. This slow journey to mastery takes time.

Companies that target new users often need to create an entirely new experience just for them. Take Jack (not his real name), a recently retired operations manager. He likes spending time with his grandson Tommy, a baseball prodigy. Jack would love to go see every one of Tommy's games, but they live several hours away from each other, so this is not an option. Instead, Tommy suggests that Jack check out the videos and photos he posts on Facebook.

Jack has never been on Facebook. He has been reluctant to join the social network because he finds the idea of a stream of spammy and irrelevant content stressful and overwhelming. He's also anxious that the experience will be unforgiving to novices and that he won't be able to navigate the network easily.

To his surprise upon downloading and trying out Facebook for the first time, Jack isn't inundated by posts, pictures, and updates he doesn't care about. He isn't even asked to fill in a profile. Instead, a brief message on an off-white screen suggests that he connect with friends. It's a lot easier than he expected.

Jack's experience is completely tailored to his level of proficiency with Facebook. The company learned from late adopters like Jack and created an entirely new experience to onboard them successfully.

Another way companies reinvent themselves in mobile is by launching new offerings. They often wrestle with this because their large functional organizations get so absorbed in the day-to-day that they lose track of what their users want. Their products stop getting better over time. It becomes an uphill battle to learn new ways of operating and innovating.

Many companies attempt to solve that problem by practicing what's called *selective insulation* of their mobile divisions. On the one hand, they make it clear who is responsible for mobile decisions. On the other hand, they encourage everyone at the company to participate in the mobile transformation.

WhatsApp is a great example of selective insulation. When Facebook acquired it in 2014, the WhatsApp team was very small.[67] Even after the acquisition was completed, it continued to operate independently.

Leading mobile browser and advertising platform Opera Software uses a similar playbook. Opera's secret sauce is its unique ability to build tools that are very fast and don't consume a lot of Internet data on a mobile phone. In the early 2000s, Opera used these ingredients to create a very efficient mobile Internet browser. If you're old enough, you may remember it. Most people in India use it to this day. In fact, it's one of the most used smartphone apps in the country.[68]

In the late 2000s, Opera Software created a new division called Opera Mediaworks and empowered the leaders of that division to completely reinvent the business. They applied a different recipe to the secret sauce and built an entirely new mobile product: one of the largest mobile video networks in the world. Today, it reaches over a billion people.

Companies sometimes need to reinvent their entire business model. Remember Clay, the contractor we discussed in chapter 3, who doubled his business when he started using Yelp? Because he did great work, he got great reviews. Customer references are the best kind of advertising. Besides, he got all of it for free. A great deal for him, of course, but that's not sustainable for a company like Yelp.

Like any business, Yelp needs to make money. It initially did so by carving out areas on its website where it could display banner advertising. On mobile, however, there is no space for banner ads because the screen is too small. Mobile banners ads are annoying rather than enticing to users.

So Yelp had to reinvent its business model. The company went back to its users and tried to understand what they would be receptive to. They learned that users have no patience when they search on the go; they want instant recommendations rather than have to scroll through dozens of reviews.

Yelp tried promoting select small businesses in its search results by placing them at the top of the list. It worked. Instead of displaying banner ads, it now charges small businesses a fee in exchange for greater visibility and better placement. Users like it better this way, and Yelp brings in revenue.

When mobile products and the companies that create them actively engage in this ongoing learning and reinventing process, everyone benefits.

Learning in Context

Companies that get really serious about learning do so in context. They focus on impact. They don't care how much effort it takes to reach their goal. They care about having more people use them so they can learn faster and get even better. They also realize that what worked a month ago no longer works today. What was enough in a given context no longer is in a different environment.

Remember real estate marketplace Trulia? It relies on a metric called *Net Promoter Score*, or NPS, to measure impact. NPS is a widespread metric in mobile.[69] It asks users a simple question—"How likely are you to recommend Trulia to a friend?"—and captures their answer on a scale of 1 to 10 (1: not at all likely, 10: very likely). If the rating is anything below 8, it assumes that users are not satisfied.

The higher its NPS, the more likely users are to recommend Trulia to a friend, so the more people will use it.

In fact, growth hacker guru Sean Ellis, who helped companies like Dropbox and Eventbrite go from zero to IPO, talks about the need to constantly reverse engineer a product in order to make it a must-have experience.

"Use NPS to understand what users might like and what they might be disappointed with," he says.[70] "If you don't nail the first experience of a user, there's usually no second experience. And then, the ongoing experience is what referrals are based on, so it's pretty critical."

The success of a new mobile product often hinges on how it is rolled out. Some companies release very gradually, first to a randomly selected 1 percent of its users, then 5 percent, and only then to all users. Others set up sandboxes where they can get things right first, before making a new offering available to all when it's finally ready.

Mobile messenger Viber, for instance, releases new features in its smaller markets first, then in its larger ones. While it isn't widely used in the US, over 100 million people around the world use Viber every month to communicate for free with friends and family. The company was acquired in 2014 by Japanese Internet giant Rakuten for close to $1 billion.[71]

One of Viber's largest markets is the United Kingdom. Because of the strategic importance of such a large market, Viber is reluctant to test new products and features there. Instead, it has identified a couple of markets that behave just like the UK, but are smaller. These markets would normally not get a large share of attention from Viber's executives, but because of their similarity to the important UK market, they have become vital test markets.

What I find interesting about Viber's approach is that it uses its own markets as sandboxes to continue to improve its offering and, at the same time, keep the majority of its users happy. Again, everyone benefits.

Learning in context means focusing on impact. It's what Trulia does with NPS. It's what Viber does with its careful use of test markets. Now let's look at how to build mobile products that learn in all the right ways to create this impact.

Building for Learning: Mobile Products as Extensions of Our Mind

Mobile products and the companies that create them must learn relentlessly. Quickly, so they adapt to our rapidly changing needs and behaviors. And slowly, so they reinvent themselves by breaking new ground.

To accomplish this, they rely on two types of tools: scientific and artistic. Scientific tools measure everything and power optimization and rapid iterations. After a while, though, they produce diminishing returns, and this is where artistic tools come in. They help mobile companies devise creative solutions to stagnant problems.

Scientific tools wire everything so it can be measured. They collect massive amounts of data that they can then analyze. The technology they use to power this is called *big data*.

My former boss Ken Rudin ran the team at Facebook that looks after big data[72]—all the analytics, optimizations, and business insights that come from it. His team constantly keeps up with technology trends such as Hadoop and deep learning in order to remain ahead of the competition.

Rudin created a weeklong training program called Data Camp, which everyone in the company can attend. This program is widely popular because it is fun and people learn interesting things there. More importantly, it spreads a data-driven approach across the entire organization. It shapes the culture to be one of incremental learning and relentless optimization.

Realistically, only a few businesses can afford to build their own scientific tools, so dozens of companies, including Mixpanel, Kochava, and Leanplum, have stepped in to offer them out of the box, as turnkey solutions.

Scientific tools also power methodologies such as *lean agile*, which are designed for rapid iterations and frequent rollout. This approach is the foundation of Steve Blank's lean start-up methodology,[73] which is designed to demonstrate empirically that there is value in a product or feature.

But scientific tools alone only get so far. After a while, they produce diminishing returns. Another type of tool is needed: artistic tools.

"Big data is as much an art as it is a science," says Rudin, Facebook's former analytics czar. "It's about business needs. If nothing changes, you've made no impact."

Rudin trains his team to ask the right questions in order to make sure they spend their time and brainpower on priorities that matter to the company.

Artistic tools are absolutely critical to the type of breakthrough success a mobile start-up needs if it has any ambition to make it big. If you work at such a place, you must learn to master artistic tools. If you on the other hand work at a large company with stringent constraints, using artistic tools may be too risky.

People often call the successful use of artistic tools by another name: luck. They underestimate artistic tools because they are less pragmatically actionable. They are under the impression that these tools aren't real.

But there is method to the madness. Artistic tools require thinking outside the box. That's much harder to do than applying a proven formula. Yet both are crucial to success.

Mobile companies recognize this, so they assign what are called *growth teams* to learn and master scientific and artistic tools.

"Growth teams integrate product and marketing together," says Uber head of supply growth Andrew Chen.[74] Product teams, they say, are very focused on building the core features that make people want to use a product. Marketing teams focus on attracting new users. The goal of a growth team is to get users to experience the core value of a product as quickly as possible.

Thinking scientifically. Thinking artistically. Emulating both sides of our brains, left and right. This is how mobile products become extensions of our mind.

Building For Learning: Scientific And Artistic Tools

To constantly learn, reinvent, and ultimately reach mastery, mobile companies rely on scientific and artistic tools.[75] Scientific tools help set a goal and track toward it. Once their effectiveness levels off, artistic tools take over. They help mobile companies think creatively about overcoming roadblocks to improvement.

Scientific tools come in two types:

- **Goals,** such as a business equation, define desired outcomes. A business's profit, for example, is a function of volume (the number of transactions) and price. This translates into a simple business equation:

$$\text{Profit} = \frac{\text{profit}}{\text{transaction}} \times \text{\# transactions}$$

Often, companies break down the number of transactions by customer because they want customers to buy multiple times from them (it's more effective to get existing customers to buy more than to acquire new ones). So their business equation has three factors instead of two. It looks like this:

$$\text{Profit} = \frac{\text{profit}}{\text{transaction}} \times \frac{\text{\# transactions}}{\text{customer}} \times \text{\# customers}$$

Mobile companies set goals that roll up into one of these three factors. Their teams focus on either increasing the number of transactions by getting existing customers to come back; increasing the number of customers by acquiring more customers; or increasing profit per transaction by raising price.

- ◆ **Funnels,** such as attribution and tracking, trace every customer interaction and identify which ones convert toward a goal and which ones don't.

Teams use them to identify gaps and try to fill them. They optimize conversion in a very systematic and methodical way.

Once their scientific tools start producing diminishing returns, mobile companies will turn to artistic tools, which are high risk/high reward. Artistic tools allow mobile teams to think outside the box and be creative when systematically looking for breakthrough opportunities.

There are three types of artistic tools:

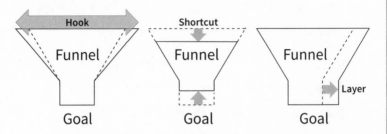

- **Hooks,** which make the top of the funnel wider, peak people's curiosity. Think about the Facebook *poke* feature or the Zillow *zestimate*. (Who doesn't want to poke a friend back or know how much their house is worth?) Hooks attract customers that would normally not have been interested. They provide a meaningful incentive for people to enter the funnel.

- **Shortcuts,** which cut a slice at the top or bottom (or both) of the funnel, remove an entire step from a user's experience. Amazon's personalized recommendations are a good example. These recommendations, labeled "other books you may like," appear immediately after a purchase. The step of searching for similar books is skipped all together.

- **Layers,** which open up a whole new layer in the funnel, create new channels that allow mobile companies to reach their customers. For example in the early days, Airbnb sourced a significant amount of its listings from Craigslist. While this wasn't legally allowed by Craigslist's terms of service, Airbnb used this layer to grow its inventory meaningfully.

  Mobile products that use scientific and artistic tools to constantly analyze, interpret, and optimize our environment act as extensions of our minds.

Building Nokia and Facebook for Learning

I implemented the learning fast/learning slow approach at both Nokia and Facebook.

Let's start with Nokia. Every morning, my entire team would get together for no more than 15 minutes. We'd review our goals, how we were tracking against them, what needed to be done next, and who would own the action items. We wouldn't focus our attention beyond what had to be done that day because we knew we would meet up again the following morning to touch base.

After two weeks of intense iterations, we'd update our product. We'd collect data about how our users received the changes we made. If they liked it, we'd plan to do more of it. If they didn't, we'd plan to course correct. Based on these early signals, we'd come up with a new set of goals for two weeks and would go back to our daily optimization.

The results of this approach were astonishing. Everything we tracked looked like the proverbial hockey stick on a growth chart. The team was so excited about the impact it was making that it worked harder and better together. It made our users happier and they would use our product more. It created a virtuous cycle. The more people used our product, the better it got. This approach is an example of scientific tools in action. It is often referred to as *agile methodology* when it is used in engineering organizations.

But at Nokia, the sales and marketing teams were also on board. The entire organization was working in unison. So instead of seeing results only at a technical level, like more predictable and higher quality product releases, we also saw a business impact: more user growth, better retention, increased revenue. It wasn't just the technology that was constantly being optimized and reinvented; it was the entire business. This approach is definitely unorthodox. It's an example of using artistic tools to foster communication and synergy.

Thanks to our outstanding results, we reached the top 1 percent of the app store. Millions of people downloaded our app. Our business unit eventually came to the attention of executives at Nokia's headquarters in Finland. They contacted me directly, curious about the secrets behind our success.

We invited them to come to San Francisco and see our team in action. It was January. We knew it was an offer they couldn't refuse: in the winter, Finland is buried under six feet of snow while San Francisco is mostly sunny.

After this visit, they invited me to discuss ways we could integrate our independent business unit into the larger organization. This eventually led to our mobile product being preloaded on every Nokia smartphone. It was a huge accomplishment for our team because at the time, two out of every five smartphones were sold by Nokia.

Nokia empowered small, nimble teams like ours, letting them learn fast and grow independently. If they were successful and the time was right, they brought them into their mainstream business units as a way to reinvent themselves.

⑊ ⑊ ⑊

Now, let's look at Facebook. In 2013, my team conducted a test to determine if Facebook users would be open to receiving push notifications.

We selected a random 1 percent of users who had opted out of receiving push notifications. We showed them a screen immediately after they sent an instant message that explained to them the benefit of push notifications. For instance, they could know immediately when their friend responded to their message. It was an example of a hook, one of the artistic tools we described earlier.

What was especially tricky about our test was how much it required from the users to be successful. Those who were interested in receiving push notifications would have to go through five separate steps in order to update their settings. None of the five steps could be skipped. And we couldn't do it for them.

Typically, mobile companies lose 90 percent of their users with each step, so we were expecting hardly anyone to go through such a painful, five-step process. It was a long shot.

To our surprise, almost one in four users went ahead and changed their settings. As soon as we found out, we expanded the reach of the test and implemented the execution machine of goal setting, tracking, improving, rinse and repeat that scientific tools power.

What I found interesting about this particular test is that it revealed a change in user preferences. As recently as six months before we ran the test, a majority of Facebook users were skeptical about push notifications so they opted out of receiving them. They weren't quite sure what they were or whether they had any value. Some felt a bit assaulted by them.

Things changed quickly when users realized that push notifications allowed them to know instantly when a friend had posted a photo of them, or sent them a message, or tagged them in a post. All of a sudden, people *wanted* push notifications. What was appropriate earlier was no longer the norm now. We had to adapt and give users another chance to decide whether or not to receive push notifications.

Remember and Share

+ Where does greatness in mobile come from? We can learn about it by looking at greatness in human beings. Some extraordinary individuals achieve what most people think is completely impossible. They reach their level of mastery by learning fast, to constantly adapt and improve, and slow, to reinvent themselves and break new ground. Mobile products, too, learn fast and slow.

+ Fast: On mobile, user behavior and technology changes at an incredibly rapid pace. Mobile companies understand that the more people use their product, the better it gets. They make sure their product scores high on the Net Promoter Score (NPS) index.

+ Slow: To keep up with the pace of innovation on mobile, companies need to reinvent themselves by reaching new users, launching new products, or inventing new business models. They have no choice.

- Mobile companies rely on two types of tools to learn from their users: scientific and artistic. Scientific tools let them test relentlessly until they find something that people want. Then, they do more of it. But at some point, this produces diminishing returns. Artistic tools let them think out of the box and create disruptive changes.

Chapter 5

The Mobile Formula in the Past, Present, and Future

TL;DR

- The mobile revolution started over 140 years ago, but it only really took off with Facebook.

- While mobile devices look cool, what people really value are the apps.

- Millennials are the architects behind the mobile revolution.

- Case studies discussed in this chapter: City of Montreal, Geminoids, Ginger.io, Nokia, Periscope, and Oculus Rift.

When Steve Jobs announced the iPhone on stage in 2007, no one at Nokia really paid attention. It didn't feel like a threat to the company. According to Nokia engineers, the technology used to create the iPhone touch screen wasn't viable.

To understand why Nokia dismissed that technology, you need to remember that the company is based in Scandinavia. Winters are very harsh and people are bundled up. They wear thick gloves and don't want to take them off to use their phones. So Nokia's *resistive* touch screens relied on pressure being applied to the screen, so they could be operated with gloves on.[76] In contrast, the iPhone *capacitive* touch screens relied on contact with the skin on users' fingertips, so they could only be touched with a bare finger.

It's easy to make mistakes when trying to predict the future. Even though I had already been in Silicon Valley for years, I too casually read about the iPhone launch and didn't foresee such a rapid convergence between computers and telephones. When I look back, it makes me smile how much I underestimated the innovative power of Silicon Valley.

My perspective today is more holistic than before, because now I have context from the past and present to inform my view of the future.

The Past: Devices That Connect People

Is there some sort of Big Bang theory behind the mobile revolution? I could take a short lens and say that the mobile revolution started with the launch of the first iPhone. But like most revolutions, the mobile revolution is a movement. A combination of many factors coming together. I could list over a dozen places where some key pieces were initiated, from Oulu, Nokia's headquarters in Finland, to Silicon Valley in Northern California or Bell Labs in Murray Hill, New Jersey, or even Milan, Thomas Edison's birthplace in Ohio.

But if I had to pick one point in time when the mobile revolution began, I would say it was over 140 years ago, and it started with Alexander Graham Bell. Aleck, as he was known in his family, developed early on a special relationship with Eliza, his deaf mother. Instead of talking to her through an ear tube, he spoke very low and very close to her head. The power of his voice created deep vibrations similar to sound waves that Eliza could actually hear. Later on, he began a career as a teacher of the deaf (he liked to call himself so) and married one of his deaf pupils.

But Aleck was also a tinkerer, and he was taking science and physics classes in the evening. His secret hope was to find a way to improve a then new technology called the telegraph, by making it accessible to deaf people.

His research gave birth to an invention that changed his life and everyone else's after him. It also made him extremely wealthy and created an entire industry. That invention? The telephone.

It took almost 100 years to go from Bell's wired landline telephones to the small wireless phones people carried around in the early 2000s. Those early mobile phones were called *candy bars* due to their rectangular shape and size. Most of them were designed, produced, and sold by Nokia.

At the time, Nokia was the fifth most beloved brand in the world.[77] When I started with them, two out of every five people who owned a mobile phone owned a Nokia phone. It was a thrilling time to work there.

The company's mission was *connecting people,* and it completely lived up to it. Nokia employees all over the world were working together to connect all sorts of people—families, friends, business associates—with awesome mobile phones.

Soon, these phones evolved into *feature phones* because they had new features, such as the ability to access the Internet, store and play music, and send text messages. Some even started to incorporate a small camera. People could take pictures directly from their phone and send them to their friends. Pointing a phone at people or landmarks in public felt a bit awkward, but it didn't matter. It was so much fun to share and connect anywhere.

Many people in the world today still use feature phones (since upgraded to include 3G and touch screen capabilities). For many of them, it's their only connection to the Internet—and that's a big deal. A staggering 97 percent of people with Internet access in developing countries say it has transformed their life, compared with 78 percent in the Western world. [78]

Companies like Google, Opera Software, and Facebook (with its Internet.org initiative) are using mobile to bring free Internet to everyone on the planet. Of course, it's important to control the influence these companies could have if they are the exclusive gateway to the Internet, but the fact is that by using mobile, they are connecting to the Internet billions of people who will never touch a computer.

These companies are effectively making the Internet a human right. Imagine a business or nonprofit trying to bring television to everyone. Would it have the same impact? I don't believe so. Television is entertainment; the Internet is a door to knowledge, to communication, and to access.

So people in the developing world get even more from mobile. It makes no difference that many of them are accessing the Internet via outdated devices. The mobile revolution still brings health, education, and wealth to these underserved populations.

First, health. Several mobile health initiatives are helping reduce pregnancy risks and infant mortality by making it easier for pregnant women in rural areas to reach hospitals. Nokia Life Tools offers not only pregnancy and child-care advice, but information and assistance on a range of health topics, including diabetes, hepatitis, and respiratory, heart, and digestive health.

Second, education. A recent study by UNESCO and Nokia[79] revealed that hundreds of thousands of people in the developing world use their mobile phone to read books. Many of them would not otherwise be able to get their hands on these books because they live in remote areas. Today, most of the content available on the Internet is in English, so the full benefit of mobile books will truly be reached once these books become digitally available in local languages.

Third, wealth. Mobile money services such as m-pesa are now available to 60 percent of the developing world.[80] They provide financial access to people who previously didn't have a bank account. Before money services, they had to buy everything in cash, or barter for it.

The mobile revolution has also sparked entrepreneurship in places like the Philippines and Vietnam. Designers, programmers, and customer support representatives from these and other countries source projects and jobs via services such as Elance and 99designs.

Because human-first principles are at the core of what great mobile is, the mobile revolution is creating a better world for everyone.

Although a lot has happened on the device side—from Alexander Bell's first telephone, to Nokia's mobile phones, to Apple's mobile computers, to smartphones—hardware is only a small part of the mobile revolution.

The Present:
Less Hardware, More Software

For mobile manufacturers like Nokia and Apple, the so-called *reason to buy* is a critical component of why phones that are pitched internally to the management team get approved or rejected.

During the era of the feature phone, the pitches would be all about hardware capabilities. They would sound like this: "People will buy this phone because it will have the best camera available on the market at its price point. Therefore we request approval to build and launch it."

In today's era of smartphones, the pitches are less about hardware and more about software. Today, people buy the phones that have their favorite apps. Apps, not high-resolution cameras, are the reason Apple and Google smartphones are so popular.

This in and of itself isn't new. The computer revolution in the 1970s and '80s was also more about software than hardware. People started buying computers and putting them in their homes not because they were cool devices, but because they had useful applications, like Microsoft Word, or games, like Pac-Man and Tetris.

Looking under the hood, at the operating-system side of software, things took a turn when Microsoft founder Bill Gates signed a very favorable deal with IBM, the industrial giant, which gave Microsoft a royalty for every sale of the software that became known as MS-DOS (Microsoft Disk Operating System). In about a decade, Microsoft captured more than 90 percent market share of the world's personal computers.[81]

The hardware side—smaller hard drives, thinner screens, improved keyboards, innovative mice—was always a significant part of the appeal of computers. But the biggest needle mover was software.

It's the same today. The mobile revolution is no longer about touch screens, cameras, and other hardware. It's about software. Netscape cofounder and Silicon Valley icon Marc Andreessen put it colorfully when he said, "Software is eating the world."[82] His partner in charge of mobile, Benedict Evans, argues that "Google's [mobile devices are] about devices as dumb glass," meaning they are mere containers for the software wonders within.

The brilliance of Steve Jobs is that he applied the Moore's law of computers (the industry he knew) to mobile phones. Moore's law is an empirical assumption that computers get smaller and smarter and cheaper all at the same time. It's counterintuitive because typically, people assume that smarter products cost more and that making things smaller, i.e., more efficient, is also more expensive. With computers and mobile phones, it's the opposite, primarily because the rate of innovation is so fast in these industries. (OK, so maybe iPhones aren't getting any cheaper, but you get my point.)

Things started accelerating when Apple and Google created an ecosystem of mobile developers. That's when mobile apps appeared. And one app in particular—Facebook—is blazing the trail for all the other apps in the mobile revolution today.

The primary reason to buy for today's smartphones is so people can check Facebook anytime. With more than a billion monthly users, Facebook is the largest social network on the planet.[83] It connects hundreds of millions of people who constantly share photos, messages, and updates about their lives.

Wouldn't you want to know immediately if, say, your sister posted a picture of her newborn daughter? Wouldn't you want to see it immediately? A Facebook user who doesn't have a mobile phone could only do so when they had access to a computer. It's more than inconvenient; it's frustrating.

Today, for every 10 minutes people spend on their smartphone, they spend at least 1 on Facebook alone.[84] For them, the mobile revolution is less about carrying around a sleek iPhone and more about being able to check Facebook.

So just as Bill Gates was considered the father of the computer revolution then, today I believe that the father of the mobile revolution is Mark Zuckerberg, the founder and CEO of Facebook.

Almost 9 out of 10 users access Facebook from a mobile device.[85] The frenzy for smartphones became even more important as services like Airbnb, Instagram, Uber, WhatsApp, and thousands of others started to launch incredibly successful mobile apps.

Some purists might argue that Facebook is an Internet company that became mobile because it went through a mobile-first transition, as we discussed in chapter 1. They may say the same about companies like Yelp, Trulia, or Amazon, that they are not mobile-first companies but instead are Internet companies because they started with a website. But the salient fact is this: two out of three current users of these companies are on mobile. And every month, these companies make more money on mobile and less everywhere else. They may have been Internet companies before, but they are very much mobile companies today.

Mobile Formula Case Study:
The Facebook Smartphone App

Because the Facebook smartphone app is built on human-first principles, it replicates and amplifies human behavior and interaction. Let's examine how it embodies the Mobile Formula.

The first characteristic is beauty. To be successful, mobile products must be beautiful. Beauty in mobile comes from efficiency, where nothing on mobile is wasted, and wow, a strong and primal emotion.

The Facebook smartphone app is so efficient and easy to operate that it's used by 20 percent of the planet. It has inspired thousands of mobile designers around the world.

The way each person experiences the app is completely unique. It tells users what their friends are up to right now. Its appeal is universal. It has created wow.

The second characteristic is meaning. Mobile products are with us always and know exactly what matters to us. Meaning from mobile comes through personalization and community.

The Facebook smartphone app knows a lot about what matters to each of us. Not a single person has the same experience on Facebook. Everyone can constantly personalize their set of friends and hobbies, what they see on their News Feed, what they post, and so on.

As for community, Facebook's mission is to make the world more open and connected. Facebook creates communities by connecting people everywhere.

The third characteristic is learning. Mobile products adapt constantly to us. They do so fast and slow. Adapting is a matter of survival.

First, fast. Inside Facebook, there is a sense of absolute urgency. The speed at which things are happening is striking. When I worked there, I'd go to a colleague and ask for information that I knew would require some effort to compile. I expected them to respond something along the lines of, "Got it. Let me work on it and get back to you in a week or two because right now, I'm wrapping up these other three projects." Instead, my colleague would say, "Wow, let me look into this right now. It might take me a couple of hours to compile the results. Is that okay? If that's too long, just let me know and I'll get someone else to help out."

And slow. The address of the Facebook headquarters is 1 Hacker Way. Hacking is a term that Silicon Valley geek culture borrowed from the phone phreak culture of the '70s and '80s. Phreaking was all about deconstructing, studying, and repurposing telephone systems. The company has made that ethos part of its own culture. Every couple of months, it hosts Hackathons, all-night coding sessions where employees create quick prototypes. The best ones are then integrated into Facebook. It makes for constant, ongoing evolution.

A Dystopian Future

So what future does the mobile revolution hold?

Some people are pessimistic. They believe that we're gradually going to be replaced by our mobile products.

In the movie *Modern Times,* Charlie Chaplin may have been one of the earliest social critics of the relentless march of industrialization.[86] In the role of his iconic Little Tramp character, he portrays a factory worker who is chosen as the guinea pig for testing a feeding machine designed to eliminate lunch breaks.

Little Tramp is strapped to a seat, fed by a mechanical arm, and regularly cleaned by an automatic mouth wiper. While everything goes smoothly at first, the machine suddenly starts to malfunction. Sparks shoot out of the motor, soup is splashed all over Little Tramp's face, and the mouth wiper hits him in the head. Although played for laughs, it is an undignified, dehumanizing scene.

Chaplin's argument is that rampant industrialization is at odds with the natural constitution of human beings. Factories strip workers of their humanity. Assembly line workers are seen as servants to machines, and they are needed only because automation cannot replace them yet.

In the summer of 2014, a hyper-realistic robot was showcased at a tradeshow in Japan.[87] The artificial woman was the latest in a remarkable series, named Geminoids by their creator, roboticist Hiroshi Ishiguro. They are a modern version of man-made creatures that aspire to become human, like Pinocchio or Frankenstein's monster.

Geminoids don't just look approximately or barely human; they look like actual humans. Representing the leading edge of mobile technology, they are the ultimate beauty.

Remember the two characteristics of beautiful mobile products? Efficiency and wow? Geminoids have both.

Geminoids are helpful to people around them, answering questions in perfect Japanese (or any other language). They come across as empathetic, blinking and fidgeting the way we humans do. And, they are modeled after real humans, with a smooth silicon skin, a friendly smile, and natural hair. They have crossed that awkward threshold called the "uncanny valley,"[88] a term coined by robotics professor Masahiro Mori to describe the revulsion people feel when they interact with something that looks almost but not exactly like a human being.

Geminoids would seem like a perfect reconstitution of Mother Nature if it wasn't for one thing they have that we never will: eternal youth. Don't you dream sometimes that you could be young forever? I certainly do.

Well, Geminoids have no such concerns. The only thing they might dream about is electric sheep, but by the time we discover that, it will be too late. They'll have taken over.

Are we at risk of gradually getting replaced and controlled by our mobile products? For now, the apocalyptic scenarios portrayed in movies like *Blade Runner*[89] and *Terminator*,[90] of a future where androids and robots have taken control, are nothing but horror tales to give us chills. But advanced AI getting out of our hands is a real and potentially serious threat, according to Stephen Hawking, Elon Musk, and several other visionaries. They're concerned that by the time we realize it, it will be too late to take action.[91]

In his book *The Question Concerning Technology*,[92] philosopher Martin Heidegger writes that we use technology to amplify our impact in and on the world. But he takes it further, explaining how technology also serves as a magnifying glass that amplifies both the good and bad sides of humans. So yes, I suppose mobile technology could have unintended consequences or, in an extreme scenario, be used for evil purposes.

But it could also be used for good, and that's where I'm placing my bets. Look, I'm a positivist. I don't have my head in the sand, but I think that mostly good things are going to spring from the mobile revolution and that we'll be able to deal with the bad things. For instance, many jobs robots do—investigating hazardous environments, cleaning industrial ducts—are extremely dangerous. Living in a society where people don't need to do them would be a good thing.

Mobile can also lead many of us to a more meaningful, rewarding work life. In her book *The Human Condition*, Heidegger's pupil, political philosopher Hannah Arendt,[93] observes how modern technology transforms our relationship to what we do: instead of working to live, we're living to work.

She encourages us to find more meaning. She distinguishes *work*, the urge we all have to make an impact and leave a mark in the world through our talent and craft, from *labor*, the need to make a living and survive. Bound to necessity, labor is alienating while work is liberating. Driven by biology, labor is the realm of animals while work is distinctly human.

I believe the mobile revolution can help us all labor less and live better. Let's explore what this future could be.

A Better Future: Millennials' Hands Are on the Tiller

Millennials, people coming of age in the twenty-first century, are shaping the future of the mobile revolution.

What sets millennials apart from other generations first and foremost is their level of proficiency with technology. They're often referred to as *digital natives*. Every day, they spend on average six hours online.[94] Already, six million of them are *smartphone dependent*. That means that one in seven of them completely depends on a smartphone for Internet access.

A study by the Pew Research Center[95] described them as *confident, connected,* and *open to change*. Let's unpack this and relate it to the Mobile Formula's rules of body, spirit, and mind.

First, millennials are confident that who they are and what is around them can be trusted, that their environment works as they expect it to. They believe that mobile products (and technology in general) make life easier and that they bring people closer to those around them. They want mobile products that just *work*, with ease of use and simplicity as a top priority. Beauty is a core value. It's the Body Rule.

What does this mean? Designers will play a critical role in creating the types of mobile products that millennials not only want but expect.[96] We've discussed that mobile design that incorporates the Body Rule relies on a whole new set of design elements—some focusing, some expanding. These design elements are the foundation not only of today's mobile products, but also of tomorrow's. Design best practices such as keeping users focused on one thing at a time, using touch extensively, and optimizing performance call for focusing design elements. Best practices for expanding design elements, including things like enabling location-aware services or allowing contextual reminders and push notifications, create offerings that make everyday life easier.

I experienced a futuristic moment when I watched a live stream of the Grateful Dead Fare Thee Well concert on Periscope last summer. Periscope is a live video streaming service that Twitter bought in the spring of 2015 for a reported $100 million. Its motto is "explore the world through someone else's eyes," and believe me, it lives up to its words. It was as if I was right there at Soldier Field in Chicago, experiencing the thrill of the music alongside the rest of the crowd.

"We think we're building a teleportation product," says Periscope founder Kayvon Beykpour.[97] He's not the only one. Several other mobile teams believe that teleportation is ready for disruption. I'm only half joking.

Entertainment experiences today are in two, maybe three dimensions. Tomorrow, they will be surround experiences, taking us places we would otherwise not dream of being. The efficiency of the advanced technologies will make it a seamless experience. The experience in turn will wow us. It will be beautiful.

Here's another futuristic example of the Body Rule in action. A group of students were recently invited to participate in a simulation inside the Virtual Human Interaction Lab at Stanford University.[98] The experiment was designed to help people combat phobias.

One of them recalls: "When the floor surrounding where I stood disappeared and I was left balancing on a narrow wooden plank some 33 feet above a pit, I struggled not to fall off the edge. I was about to hyperventilate. In reality my feet were firmly planted on the ground, but my brain was tricked into believing I was suspended."

He was wearing Oculus Rift, the new mobile headgear recently acquired by Facebook, and wanted to overcome his fear of heights.

In this lab, visitors are invited to try many more of these immersive experiences. Some let you see an alternate reflection of yourself in a virtual mirror. You become someone you're not: a woman, an elder, or a person of color. The demo includes other avatars that throw abusive stereotypes at you. The intent is to make you more empathetic toward others.

Other stations in the lab are meant to help you be more resilient to pain, better manage your money, live a healthier lifestyle, and more.

The common thread is that, rather than relying on photos or video, the lab uses mobile technology to allow users to share entire immersive experiences. Not unlike what happens to the characters in the movie *Avatar*, it teleports them into an entirely new environment that becomes their virtual reality.

This new form of entertainment and expanding our boundaries could help people connect more intimately and understand each other better. It could create perspective and empathy. It could make us more trusting and confident. It shows us the power of the Body Rule.

Second, more than any other generation, millennials are connected all the time. They expect their mobile products to help them deal with the things that bother them so that they can focus on what's important to them, on what gives them meaning. They want their mobile products to sort through the fire hose of information they are bombarded with by being highly personalized. They demand help to make everyday decisions. They need a way to find meaning from information overload. This is the Spirit Rule.

What does this mean? Author and user experience visionary Mike Kuniavsky predicts that our devices themselves are becoming avatars,[99] our mobile alter egos. He distinguishes appliances like a fridge or computer, both of which we have to operate manually, from devices like smartphones, which are able to act on their own. Smart devices know a lot about us and can transform this knowledge into actions.

"Your tiny, wimpy device . . . can be effectively as powerful as the world's most powerful computer," says Kuniavsky. As a result, our relationship to our devices is changing. They are becoming avatars—extensions of us.

Tomorrow, argues Kuniavsky, every device will be smart. In fact, Goldman Sachs predicts that there will be 28 billion smart devices by 2020.[100] That's four devices for every one person on the planet. Companies like Google and Apple are already extending their mobile platforms to support every possible device, a mobile trend known as the Internet of Things. Kuniavsky advises top companies such as Samsung, Sony, Whirlpool, and Qualcomm to get ready for this too because their platforms will soon use the personalization and community filters we discussed in chapter 3 to power entire cities.[101]

The City of Montreal gives us a glimpse of what the city of the future could look like. It created a smartphone app that combined public transportation information with local offers from shops in the vicinity of subway stations. As commuters got off the train, they were presented with a personalized offer like a discount at the flower store around the corner, or a coupon for a pizzeria next door. Soon, people started going on shopping sprees. In fact, 15 percent of the offers that merchants put out were redeemed. That's five to eight times the typical conversion rate of local coupons and offers. Merchants started asking the city to deploy the program more broadly.

The city also wanted to find ways to reduce pollution and congestion in order to improve quality of life. It created a mobile game called Save the Trees. Every time people took a trip into the city using public transportation instead of their own vehicles, they saved energy. The energy savings per trip is approximately equivalent to the energy created by burning a tree. So the game rewarded commuters with one virtual tree for every trip. This gave citizens a way to create communities that care about the environment.

These pilot programs were so successful that the Montreal is expanding its public transportation infrastructure and looking for other ways to use personalization and community to better the lives of its citizens and visitors by connecting them to the things that matter to them.

Of course, there are many other factors to consider before cities become smart, including regulatory and security requirements. But think for a moment about the possibilities of the Spirit Rule—achieving what matters to us through personalization and community—at the scale of an entire connected city. The possibilities for personal transportation alone are exciting: Traffic self-regulating without traffic lights. Accidents detected instantly, improving the effectiveness of emergency services. Connected cars driving us around, refilling their own gas tank or recharging their own batteries, parking themselves, maintaining themselves. It would not only make our roads and cities safer, it would make our lives exponentially easier.

Third, being open to change means that millennials want their mobile products to learn alongside them. They want them to adapt according to the Mind Rule.

Take an issue like health care. This is particularly important to millennials because more than any other generation, they are victims of chronic diseases such as obesity and diabetes. Companies spend huge amounts to promote weight loss programs, smoking cures, and other efforts to address unhealthy conditions and lifestyles.

Mobile products could power a revolutionary new approach to health care.[102] Because they are with us always, they can learn from us in real time. This enables them to monitor chronic diseases and other health problems.

Apple, Samsung, and other mobile platforms have started to offer ways for people to automatically track their health data, such as heart rate. People can share it with their doctors if they want to. Several hospitals around the country have already agreed to conduct pilot programs. For instance, a doctor can be notified if a patient's heart rate becomes erratic, potentially signaling a heart emergency.

Ginger.io, a Silicon Valley start-up, uses the data patients share from Apple HealthKit and combines it with other information, such as their location or whom they call, to proactively diagnose people who might be suffering from mental health disorders. For instance, Ginger.io might notice that someone had been home all day for a few days and stopped calling a loved one or sending e-mails. Suspecting the person might be suffering from early symptoms of depression, it automatically notifies their doctor.

Researchers at the City University of New York use smartphones to better understand the risks posed to public health by illicit drugs. They conduct experiments where they loan smartphones to a group of drug addicts in order to collect information about their addiction. From the data they collect, they create mathematical models that can predict how diseases like AIDS or hepatitis are likely to spread as a result of drug consumption in the community. They use their findings to make recommendations to such health organizations as the National Health Foundation. Their research helps decide how tax dollars should be allocated and what programs to prioritize to limit the spread of fatal diseases in our cities.

Mobile products could transform the way we do medical research. Medidata, a software company that facilitates clinical trials, has started to use smart devices to get new drugs to market faster. Instead of asking patients to come in for a checkup, say, once a month during a clinical trial, they provide them with a mobile device that tracks key health indicators continuously. This approach considerably accelerates Federal Drug Administration approvals so new drugs are available faster to the general public.

Of course, there are many obstacles to overcome on the way to better health care. But as we stay open to change and keep learning and adapting, the Mind Rule will help us create mobile products that can in turn help alleviate many of the problems that plague modern society—overeating, addiction, sexually transmitted diseases, unwanted pregnancy, depression . . . the possibilities are endless.

Remember and Share

- The mobile revolution began more than 140 years ago with the invention of the telephone, but things accelerated considerably over the past 10 years.

- Paradoxically, mobile devices are only a small part of the mobile revolution: the reason millions of people around the world buy smartphones is that they want to use Facebook. People value Facebook and other apps on their smartphones far more than they value the device itself.

- Millennials show us the opportunities that the mobile revolution could bring about in the future. They want mobile products in their image: confident, connected, and open to change. Applying the Mobile Formula to future products will bring about new forms of gorgeous entertainments, useful learning opportunities, personalized experiences in connected cities, constant health monitoring and better treatments, and much more.

Conclusion

It's Your Turn Now

Now that you have an understanding of the mobile revolution, let's get to work. How can you make your own mobile product successful?

If you already have a mobile product, test it against the Mobile Formula. The Mobile Formula is "it," folks. It's all encompassing. It fits together cohesively.

Remember what we said earlier: what we wish for ourselves as human beings is what we wish for our best mobile products. We want those products to look beautiful, to help us focus on the things that matter to us, and to constantly adapt to our environment. Isn't that what we want for ourselves, too? An attractive body, a meaningful impact, and a masterful mind? Body, spirit, mind—what else is there?

However, reality is the ultimate truth, and only users decide what works for them. You can only focus on improvement in your product if you can spot the gaps in your product.

Does your product pass the thumb test? Are you using personalization to make your users' daily lives less stressful? Do you have a systematic way to receive and incorporate feedback into your product? Those and many others are the sorts of questions you need to be asking yourself and your team.

Revisit this book's Remember and Share sections. They should give you a framework for identifying gaps and areas of improvement.

If you are just getting started building a product, where might you start to transform your business and make it mobile?

To answer this question, I'm going to discuss two case studies: Uber and Sonos.

Uber is the darling of the mobile revolution and one of the leaders of the sharing economy. We'll see how it has nailed the Mobile Formula.

Sonos, a fabulous music and sound system for the home, doesn't seem at first like a mobile product. However, the company has transformed its product from a music device into a mobile-first offering. The main reason people buy it is because they can operate it from their smartphones. It makes listening to and discovering new music every day a pleasure.

What about your company? How can you think of it as a mobile-first business? In business, there are no guarantees. Lots of things must go right for a new business to succeed, and building a great mobile product is just one of them.

⫙ ⫙ ⫙

Let's run Uber's design through the Body Rule: beauty. Uber is one of the most beautiful smartphone apps out there. It clearly passes the thumb test: it's well laid out, and there is no wasted space or overly crowded area. It employs focusing design elements to make using it super simple and easy. When I signed up, the tutorial made it very clear when and why I would find Uber useful. And it only took a couple of taps to enter a destination and order my first car. Uber also uses expanding design elements. For instance, it asked me for permission to use my base location before I finished signing up. Knowing my location is necessary for Uber to personalize my experience. As a result, Uber is completely integrated in its environment. It works everywhere.

The Sonos speakers, too, have a gorgeous design, as does the app that controls the entire system. The first time I started using it, I was in awe. I was sitting on the couch and all my music was right in front of me, on my smartphone. My mother came to visit me soon after that day and played with my Sonos. She loved it so much that she bought one for herself. I'd say Sonos passes the mom test with high marks. It's beautiful.

We discussed that beauty in mobile comes from efficiency and wow. Is your product efficient? Does it pass the thumb test? Does it wow your users? How does it score on the mom test? Is it easy to operate in any environment? What are the focusing design elements you can use to help your users focus? What about expanding elements? Go back to the examples we discussed in chapter 2 to learn from the successful pioneers what makes well-designed mobile products beautiful.

How does Uber fare with the Spirit Rule—meaning? The best mobile products are with us every day, so they should do what they can to make our lives easier. Uber makes it easier for us to get to the places we need to be. For many people, it's a lifesaver. They no longer use their car to commute to work. They get to work relaxed and energized. (Remember how stressful it was for me to get a cab on a rainy day?) They feel taken care of. On the way, they even meet new people, drivers or passengers. They join the growing community of ride sharers.

Sonos partners with thousands of radio stations around the world, so I can listen to French radio in just a couple of taps and feel connected with people in my native country. I can also link Sonos to my Pandora account to play my personalized channels on the high-quality speakers without having to get up and walk to my computer. What a treat! Listening to music is now pure pleasure and no stress.

Meaning from mobile comes through personalization and community. Which of the internal filters we discussed would you use to make your users' experience personalized? What about external filters? What compromises do you need your users to make in order to comply with the social norms of the group? What can you do to make them feel like they belong?

Last, let's see what's up with Uber and the Mind Rule: learning. Great mobile products get better with time. The people behind Uber comprise one of the most ambitious teams I've ever met. They constantly observe how their users like to use Uber, how their behavior changes from one month (or day) to the next.

Some people may recall that Uber started as a high-end black car service. Then it expanded to offer a taxi service and, soon after, a carpooling service. It started in San Francisco; it's now operating in dozens of cities. As if this wasn't enough, Uber realized that people wanted more door-to-door services than just a car pick-up, so it recently started to offer food delivery. It's hard to find a company that matches Uber's level of mastery.

Sonos, too, has embraced the Mind Rule and taken to heart the cultural transformation that becoming mobile-first requires. It now operates like a mobile-first company, with a big back office that handles a whole lot of things such as logistics and device manufacturing.

What about your company and the Mind Rule? Regardless of the maturity of your business right now, you continually need to find ways to adapt if you want to survive. Are you rewarding impact and results over effort? Have you implemented iterative processes such as agile methodologies? Maybe you need a growth team to help you keep up with the pace of innovation? Consider the examples and the approaches that work to achieve mastery at scale and at speed.

It goes beyond smartphones and their apps. Mobile products will soon be embedded into our clothes, jewelry, watches, and glasses. Are any of those products on your drafting table? Like Uber's ridesharing and Sonos's music system, they'll still have to observe the Mobile Formula's three rules to connect with our humanness and be successful.

I have no doubt the mobile revolution will change our lives for the better. Remember what I said at the beginning: this book may seem like a book on technology, but really, it's a book about humans. Great mobile products replicate and amplify human behavior and interaction.

The Mobile Formula is based on an unyielding attention to humanity as opposed to the machines that serve it. Always remember that.

Have fun. And good luck.

Notes

1. http://money.cnn.com/2014/02/28/technology/mobile/mobile-apps-internet

2. http://www.wsj.com/articles/SB10001424053111903480904576512250915629460

3. http://www.huffingtonpost.com/sophiecharlotte-moatti/building-mobile-products-_b_8918348.html"

4. http://www.pewresearch.org/daily-number/do-you-sleep-with-your-cell-phone

5. http://www.emeraldinsight.com/doi/abs/10.1108/13522751111137497

6. https://en.wikipedia.org/wiki/Conspiracy_For_Good and http://online.wsj.com/news/articles/SB10001424052748703904304575497473735761294

7. Books covering some aspects of the mobile revolution include Libert, B. (2013). *The mobile revolution*; Majeed, A. (2011). *Smartphone: Mobile revolution at the crossroads of communications, computing and consumer electronics.* North Charleston, South Carolina: CreateSpace; Pearson, A. (2009). *The mobile revolution.* Miami, FL: Qualex Consulting Services.

   Articles covering some aspects of the mobile revolution include:

   "Vital Signs 2003 Current Trends." *New Scientist* 178, no. 2396 (05/24, 2003): 8. http://search.ebscohost.com.libaccess.sjlibrary.org/login.aspx?direct=true&db=a9h&AN=9957457&site=ehost-live.

   Beasty, Colin. "The Mobile Revolution Rings True." *CRM Magazine* 9, no. 10 (10, 2005): 20–20. http://search.ebscohost .com.libaccess.sjlibrary.org/login.aspx?direct

=true&db=a9h&AN=18605239&site=ehost-live.

Chisnall, Peter M. "The Mobile Revolution: The Making of Mobile Services Worldwide." *International Journal of Market Research* 49, no. 2 (03, 2007): 275–276. http://search.ebscohost.com.libaccess.sjlibrary.org/login.aspx?direct=true&db=bth&AN=24258551&site=ehost-live.

Douglas, Jeanne-Vida. "The Mobile Revolution." *Brw* 31, no. 18 (05/07, 2009): 32–34. http://search.ebscohost.com.libaccess.sjlibrary.org/login.aspx?direct=true&db=a9h&AN=41786736&site=ehost-live.

Gallagher, Matt. "The Mobile Revolution." *Red Herring* (08/03/2010): 12–12. http://search.ebscohost.com.libaccess.sjlibrary.org/login.aspx?direct=true&db=a9h&AN=52707178&site=ehost-live.

Grant, Ian. "The Mobile Revolution: The Making of Mobile Services Worldwide." *International Journal of Advertising* 25, no. (02, 2006): 119–120. http://search.ebscohost.com.libaccess.sjlibrary.org/login.aspx?direct=true&db=ufh&AN=19754854&site=ehost-live.

Johnson, N. J. "The Mobile Revolution: The Making of Mobile Services Worldwide." *Choice: Current Reviews for Academic Libraries* 43, no. 8 (04, 2006): 1450–1450. http://search.ebscohost.com.libaccess.sjlibrary.org/login.aspx?direct=true&db=ehh&AN=20676279&site=ehost-live.

Logan, Mary K. "A Roundtable Discussion: Embracing the Mobile Revolution." *Biomedical Instrumentation & Technology* (09/02, 2012): 10–17 8p. http://search.ebscohost.com.libaccess.sjlibrary.org/login.aspx?direct=true&db=ccm&AN=108102788&site=ehost-live.

Merina, Anita. "Managing the Technology Takeover." *NEA Today* (Summer 2013, 2013): 16–16.

http://search.ebscohost.com.libaccess.sjlibrary.org/
login.aspx?direct=true&db=a9h&AN=93985859&site
=ehost-live.

Ozimek, John. "The Mobile Revolution." *Journal of Database Marketing & Customer Strategy Management* 12, no. 4 (07, 2005): 378–379. http://search.ebscohost.com.
libaccess.sjlibrary.org/login.aspx?direct=true&db
=bth&AN=17452960&site=ehost-live.

Ray, Subhjayoti. "The Mobile Revolution." *Economic & Political Weekly* 48, no. 23 (06/08, 2013): 28–30.
http://search.ebscohost.com.libaccess.sjlibrary.org/
login.aspx?direct=true&db=poh&AN=101194387&site
=ehost-live.

Treweek, S. "Joining the Mobile Revolution." *Scandinavian Journal of Primary Health Care* 21, no. 2 (06, 2003): 75–75 1p. http://search.ebscohost.com.libaccess.sjlibrary.org/
login.aspx?direct=true&db=ccm&AN=106103312&site
=ehost-live.

Treweek, Shaun. "Joining the Mobile Revolution."
Scandinavian Journal of Primary Health Care 21, no. 2 (06, 2003): 75. http://search.ebscohost.com.libaccess.
sjlibrary.org/login.aspx?direct=true&db=a9h&AN
=9755830&site=ehost-live.

Wirbel, Loring. "The Mobile Revolution. (Cover Story)."
Electronic Engineering Times (01921541) no. 785 (02/21, 1994): 35. http://search.ebscohost.com.libaccess.sjlibrary
.org/login.aspx?direct=true&db=a9h&AN=9408023987
&site=ehost-live.

7. https://www.bcgperspectives.com/content/articles/
telecommunications_technology_business_transformation
_mobile_revolution

8. http://www.smartinsights.com/mobile-marketing/mobile
-marketing-analytics/mobile-marketing-statistics

9. http://www.forbes.com/sites/markpmills/2015/01/19
   /the-mobile-revolution-has-only-just-begun

10. http://www.paulgraham.com/yahoo.html

11. http://www.slideshare.net/jeremiah_owyang/a-day-in-the
    -life-of-the-collaborative-economy

12. http://www.nielsen.com/us/en/insights/reports/2014/is
    -sharing-the-new-buying.html

13. http://www.bbc.com/news/business-30442712

14. https://hbr.org/2015/03/the-sharing-economys-new
    -middlemen

15. https://en.wikipedia.org/wiki/Fordism

16. https://sherpashare.com/share/2014-in-review-the-top-6
    -rideshare-driver-trends

17. http://www.forbes.com/sites/ericjackson/2012/06/12/why
    -facebook-doesnt-have-mobile-in-its-founding-dna-and
    -why-that-spells-disaster

18. http://productsthatcount.com/2015/01/
    video-jocelyn-goldfein-form-follows-function

19. http://www.huffingtonpost.com/sophiecharlotte-moatti
    /become-a-mobilefirst-comp_b_5353964.html

20. https://en.wikipedia.org/wiki/Golden_mean

21. http://www.dailymail.co.uk/sciencetech/article-2449632
    /How-check-phone-The-average-person-does-110-times
    -DAY-6-seconds-evening.html

22. https://www.sciencenews.org/article/measure-beauty

23. http://smile.amazon.com/Aesthetic-Measure-George-David
    -Birkhoff/dp/0674730224

24. https://www.youtube.com/watch?v=9hUIxyE2Ns8

25. http://www.pandora.com

26. https://en.wikipedia.org/wiki/Music_Genome_Project

27. https://instagram.com/press

28. http://www.hongkiat.com/blog/most-expensive-tech
 -acquisitions

29. http://www.greenowlmobile.com/

30. http://www.goldenkrishna.com

31. https://en.wikipedia.org/wiki/Amazon_Echo

32. https://claralabs.com

33. https://en.wikipedia.org/wiki/What_Is_Art%3F

34. https://flipboard.com

35. http://www.theatlantic.com/technology/archive/2013/07
 /the-mom-test/277482

36. https://airbnb.com

37. http://joegebbia.com

38. http://www.fastcodesign.com/1670890/how-airbnb
 -evolved-to-focus-on-social-rather-than-searches#1

39. http://knockknock.co

40. http://www.fastcodesign.com/1671237/frog-creates-an
 -open-source-guide-to-design-thinking

41. http://productsthatcount.com/2015/09/99-design-guru
 -joe-robinson-on-tech-design-trends

42. https://slack.com

43. http://www.fastcompany.com/3042326/tech-forecast/with-
 500000-users-slack-says-its-the-fastest-growing-business
 -app-ever

44. www.flickr.com

45. https://stripe.com

46. http://www.huffingtonpost.com/sophiecharlotte-moatti
 /the-7-design-elements-of-great-mobile-products_b
 _8175942.html

47. https://en.wikipedia.org/wiki/Hay_Day

48. https://en.wikipedia.org/wiki/Her_(film)

49. http://www.apa.org/monitor/2012/01/self-control.aspx

50. https://en.wikipedia.org/wiki/Tinder_(app) and
    http://time.com/4837/tinder-meet-the-guys-who-turned
    -dating-into-an-addiction/ and http://time.com/4799/the
    -new-dating-game/ and http://www.gq.com/story/tinder
    -online-dating-sex-app and http://www.news.com.au
    /finance/business/the-real-story-behind-hugely-successful
    -dating-app-tinder/story-fn5lic6c-1226856885645

51. http://productsthatcount.com/2015/05/5-27-nir-eyal
    -building-habit-forming-products

52. http://ufdcimages.uflib.ufl.edu/UF/E0/04/35/17/00001/Park
    _K.pdf

53. http://www.scientificamerican.com/article/how-the
    -illusion-of-being-observed-can-make-you-better-person

54. http://www.macworld.co.uk/news/iosapps/does-anyone
    -actually-use-siri-10-things-about-siri-make-it-
    worthwhile-3489208

55. https://en.wikipedia.org/wiki/CALO

56. https://en.wikipedia.org/wiki/Behavioral_economics and
    http://danariely.com/tag/behavioral-economics-2

57. http://www.huffingtonpost.com/sophiecharlotte-moatti
    /the-five-personalization-_b_8805538.html

58. https://en.wikipedia.org/wiki/Yelp

59. http://www.hbs.edu/faculty/Publication%20Files/12-016
    _0464f20e-35b2-492e-a328-fb14a325f718.pdf

60. http://www.yelp.com/factsheet

61. http://goinswriter.com/robert-greene-mastery

62. http://www.history.co.uk/biographies/nelson-mandela

63. http://productsthatcount.com/2014/06/video-kristen
    -berman-building-great-products-using-the-insights-of
    -irrationality

64. http://www.quora.com/Why-do-people-like-Whatsapp-so
    -much-What-makes-it-better-than-Facebook-Messenger and
    http://www.wired.com/2014/02/whatsapp-rules-rest-world

65. https://www.facebook.com/photo.php?fbid
=10102273327714831&set=a.529237706231.2034669.4
&type=1&theater

66. http://productsthatcount.com/2015/04/video-sami
-inkinen-how-to-achieve-the-impossible

67. http://sequoiacapital.tumblr.com/post/77211282835/four
-numbers-that-explain-why-facebook-acquired

68. http://blogs.opera.com/india/2015/05/opera-mini-top
-android-app-in-india-says-mary-meekers-2015-internet
-trends-report

69. https://www.netpromoter.com/know

70. http://productsthatcount.com/2015/09/930-growth-guru
-sean-ellis-on-products-meets-growth

71. http://www.bloomberg.com/news/articles/2014-02-17
/rakuten-falls-on-900-million-deal-to-acquire-viber
-message-app

72. http://productsthatcount.com/2015/05/623-facebook
-analytics-vp-on-big-data-bigger-impact

73. https://en.wikipedia.org/wiki/Steve_Blank#Lean_Startup
_Movement

74. http://www.coelevate.com/essays/growth-vs-marketing
-vs-product and http://www.coelevate.com/essays/product
-market-fit

75. http://www.huffingtonpost.com/sophiecharlotte-moatti
/three-deceptively-simple-_b_8334508.html

76. http://www.goodgearguide.com.au/article/355922
/capacitive_vs_resistive_touchscreens

77. http://www.rankingthebrands.com/The-Brand-Rankings
.aspx?rankingID=37&year=38

78. http://www.mobileindustryreview.com/2015/05/mobile-
technology-developing-nations.html

79. http://time.com/74584/unesco-study-mobile-phones
-book-reading-literacy

80. http://www.mobileindustryreview.com/2015/05/mobile
-technology-developing-nations.html

81. http://www.historylink.org/index.cfm?DisplayPage =output
.cfm&file_id=2294

82. http://www.wsj.com/articles
/SB10001424053111903480904576512250915629460 and
http://ben-evans.com/benedictevans/2014/7/3
/the-next-phase-of-smartphones

83. http://www.statista.com/statistics/264810/number-of
-monthly-active-facebook-users-worldwide

84. http://marketingland.com/report-mobile-users-spend-80
-percent-time-just-five-apps-116858

85. http://www.adweek.com/news/technology/facebooks
-mobile-base-1-billion-users-bigger-all-twitter-166168

86. https://en.wikipedia.org/wiki/Modern_Times_(film)

87. https://www.youtube.com/watch?v=fXaaprU9DhY and
https://www.youtube.com/watch?v=IhVu2hxm07E

88. https://en.wikipedia.org/wiki/Uncanny_valley

89. http://www.imdb.com/title/tt0083658

90. http://www.imdb.com/title/tt0088247

91. http://time.com/3614349/artificial-intelligence-singularity
-stephen-hawking-elon-musk

92. https://en.wikipedia.org/wiki/The_Question_Concerning
_Technology and https://en.wikipedia.org/wiki/Gestell

93. https://en.wikipedia.org/wiki/Hannah_Arendt#Works and
http://www.iep.utm.edu/arendt/ and http://plato.stanford
.edu/entries/arendt

94. Millennial Survey: Global Results, Telefonica, 2013, and
http://www.pewinternet.org/fact-sheets/mobile
-technology-fact-sheetand http://money.cnn.com
/interactive/economy/diversity-millennials-boomers

95. Millennials, A Portrait of Generation Next, Pew Research
Center, 2010.

Notes

96. http://www.huffingtonpost.com/sophiecharlotte
    -moatti/3-best-practices-to-get-c_b_5910572.html

97. http://www.theguardian.com/technology/2015/mar/26
    /periscope-review-twitter-live-streaming-service-meerkat

98. http://www.usatoday.com/story/tech/columnist/bai /2015
    /06/16/stanford-vr-lab-overcome-fear-reduce-prejudice
    /28805611

99. http://productsthatcount.com/2014/09/video-mike
    -kuniavsky-cloud-meets-internet-of-things

100. http://www.goldmansachs.com/our-thinking/outlook
     /internet-of-things/iot-report.pdf

101. http://www.huffingtonpost.com/sophiecharlotte-moatti
     /after-mobile-3-opportunit_b_6702824.html

102. http://www.huffingtonpost.com/sophiecharlotte-moatti
     /how-the-internet-of-thing_2_b_6818982.html

Acknowledgments

Writing a book is something I've always wanted to do. As a high school student in Paris, France, I dabbled in literature before following a scientific path. Little did I know that the people around me, my friends and colleagues, would bring me back to this early dream of mine. I could never have hoped for a more supportive, inspiring group who constantly challenged me and brought the best out of me.

I'm particularly grateful to my multicultural family, who exposed me to the big and wonderful world we live in, and raised me to remain open-minded and take bold stands. My wonderful mother, Brigitte Duval, who wrote the first English method for primary school kids in France; my late father, Georges Alain Moatti, a force of nature in the face of civil war and chronic illness; my late aunt Louise Moatti, a powerful and independent woman to whom this book is dedicated; my late grandfather, Pierre Duval, a brilliant engineer who believed in me before I could even walk—all have my deepest love.

Special thanks to my wonderful life partner, Matt Houston, who never ceases to amaze me by living life to the fullest and who makes me feel loved unconditionally.

Thank you to Alexandra Watkins, without whom this book would not exist; to Mark Levy, Christian Clough, and Ran Liu, who helped me shape the manuscript; and to Nir Eyal, who wrote the foreword.

Thank you to Jeevan Sivasubramaniam and the supportive Berrett-Koehler Publishers team—I am honored to be one of your authors.

Thank you to Chris Anderson, Alexei Andreiev, Dan Arieli, Dan Arkind, Jonathan Badeen, Bogomil Balkansky, Sigal Bareket, Jamie Barnett, Roy Baumeister, Kenneth Berger, Kristen Berman, Kayvon Beykpour, Bruno Bilik, Ali Binazir, Andrew Burtis, Noah Blumenthal, Stewart Butterfield, Will Cathcart, Tim Chang, Andrew Chen, Rose Chen, John Choate, Sangeet-Paul Choudary, Charles de Coquet, Chris Cox, Charlie Crocker, Sean Dugan, Benedict Evans, Clark Freshman, James Friedman, Gaurav Hardikar, Joe Gebbia, Michel Gelobter, Marie-Laure Goepfer, Jocelyn Goldfein, Barry Grant, Robert Greene, Howard Ho, Ethan Imboden, Sami Inkinen, Alexandra Ivacheff, Robbie Kellman-Baxter, Golden Krishna, Yann Kronberg, Mike Kuniavsky, Reza Ladchartabi, Jaron Lanier, James Lattin, Loan Le, Bastian Lehman, Geraldine Le Meur, Grant Lindsay, Brian Long, Alexis Longinotti, Matt Man, Jonathan Mayer, John Maull, Mike McCues, Lull Mengesha, Lisa Miller, Bill Miranda, Mary Mookini, Rich Mironov, Sverre Munck, Tara-Nicholle Nelson, Michele Morrison,

Acknowledgments

Chris Neumann, Julia Nguyen, Kathy Nicholson, Tero Ojanpera, Dan Olsen, Jeremiah Owyang, Joseph Perla, Thomas Piketty, Herve Pluche, Scott Rafer, Joe Robinson, Patricia Roller, Dan Rubinstein, Ken Rudin, Camille Sanandaji, Carol Sands, Jill Schaeffer-Hetherington, Philipp Schloter, Eric Setton, Hiten Shah, Peter Shin, Julia Shur, Eric Singley, Ed Simnett, Fidji Simo, Chloe Sladden, Lael Sturm, Karl Sluis, Paul Tyma, Sigurt Ulland, Kira Wampler, Amy Wilkinson, David Wygant, and Mark Zuckerberg.

Thank you to Benjamin Abou, Gabriel Aractingi, Hannah Arendt, Simone de Beauvoir, Albert Camus, Albert Cohen, Jean-Michel Detavernier, Nicolas Gogol, Steve Jobs, Milan Kundera, Yukio Mishima, Emile Moatti, Bernard Nivollet, and Deep Sahni.

Thank you to the loyal members of Products That Count, who provided insightful feedback and moral support.

Finally, thank you to everyone who reads this book. You rock!

Index

A

Aesthetic Measure (Birkhoff), 41
AI (artificial intelligence)
    assistants, 64, 76
    CALO project, 77
    intersecting fields, 8
    threat factors, 130–131
Airbnb
    beauty of, 39, 49
    layers used by, 110
    origin of, 48–49
    reason for using, 25
    smartphone use and, 125–126
    successful app launch, 126
    wow factor in, 48–49
Alibaba, 22
Amazon, 8, 126
    shortcuts tool, 109
    warehouses, 24
Amazon Echo, 45
Andreessen, Marc, 124
Andressen Horowitz, 7
Android, 18
Apple
    iPhone, beauty of, 41
    Jobs' iPhone announcement, 42,
      117
    market risks taken by, 4
    mobile apps, quality controls, 28
    mobile developer ecosystem at,
      124–125
    mobile platform expansion, 136
    reason to buy component of, 123
    See also iPhone; Siri
apps. *See* mobile apps
Arendt, Hannah, 131–132

Ariely, Dan, 79
artistic tools, in building for learning
    growth teams' mastery of, 107
    hooks, 109
    importance of, 106–107
    layers, 110
    shortcuts, 109
Autodesk, 7

B

baby boomers, 75
banking services, mobile, 122
Baumeister, Roy, 66
beauty
    in ancient Greece, 39–40, 46
    building for, 53–58
    confounding nature of, 39
    in context, 50–52
    efficiency and, 39–46
    in Flipboard design, 47–48
    in France, 18th-century, 40–41
    in GreenOwl design, 45
    in Instagram, 44, 59–61
    in iPhone design, 41, 42, 50–51
    in medieval China, 36, 41–42
    in mobile product design, 42–61
    mom test of, 37, 47–48, 62,
      145–146
    in Pandora design, 43
    in Sonos speakers design, 145
    thumb test and, 62
    in Uber design, 145
    wow factor/visceral quality of,
      46–50
Bell, Alexander Graham, 119, 122
Beykpour, Kayvon, 134

big data (analytical tool), 105, 106
Birkhoff, George David, 41
blogs/blogging, 4, 8
Body Rule
    beauty and, 33, 37–62, 133
    description, 33
    design elements of, 133
    futuristic example of, 134–135
    millennials and, 133–135
    relation to mobile products, 13, 36
    Sonos and, 145
    Uber and, 145
    See also beauty
Boston Consulting Group (BCG), 13
Breeze, car-leasing service, 24
Butterfield, Stewart, 51

C
CALO (Cognitive Assistant that
    Learns and Organizes) project,
    77
Chen, Andrew, 107
Clara, 46
community
    Facebook and, 127
    meaning and, 63, 71–76, 127, 147
    power organizer organization of,
    25
    privacy concerns of, 73–75, 90
    of ride sharers, 146
    social norms and, 63, 71–76, 90
    Spirit Rule and, 34, 138
computer revolution, 123
context
    in beauty, 50–52
    in learning, 102–104
    in meaning, 76–81
cultural transformation, 28–30

D
Data Camp training program, 105
dating app development, 5

decision fatigue, 68
design of mobile products
    beauty elements, 41–42, 53–58
    external filters, 81–85, 87–88, 90,
    147
    gestures, 57
    internal filters, 67, 81, 83–84,
    86–87, 90, 147
    mom test in, 37, 47–48, 62,
    145–146
    navigation, 56–57
    onboarding, 56
    performance, 57
    pull and push, 58
    single-task, 56
    thumb test in, 37, 42–43, 45, 56,
    62, 144–146
digital advertising, 15
digital natives. *See* millennials
Dropbox, 103

E
e-commerce, 20
Elance, 122
Ellis, Sean, 103
entrepreneurs
    excitement about mobile, 7
    global span of, 122
    persistence of, 93
    sharing economy creations, 13,
    23–27
Evans, Benedict, 124
Eventbrite, 103
external filters
    forms of, 82
    meaning and, 81–84
    permission, 85
    policy, 83, 84–85
    popularity, 85, 89
    role of, 81, 82, 90
    social norms and, 82, 85, 147
    transparency and, 83

user personalization and, 147
Yelp's use of, 87–88
Eyal, Nir, 71–72

F
Facebook, 5–7, 9
    acquisition of Oculus Rift, 134
    big data analysis on, 105
    building for learning in, 112–114
    building for meaning in, 86–87
    community mission of, 127
    complaint filing process, 78–80
    content producers, 86–87
    core values at, 28, 29
    digital advertising on, 15
    free Internet access from, 120–121
    Instagram sharing on, 60
    mobile access development, 6
    mobile-first transition, 28–29
    purchase of Instagram, 44
    reaching consumers through, 15
    smartphone app, case study,
        126–128
    social mission of, 92
    strategic acquisitions, 29
    targeting of new users, 99
    Tinder interface with, 67
    updating/push notifications, 58
    user usage data, 125
Facebook Connect, 67
Facebook Login, 55
Facebook News Feed, 86
feature phones, 120
filters. *See* external filters; internal
    filters
Flipboard, 7, 47–48
Fordism, 26–27

G
Gates, Bill, 125
Gebbia, Joe, 48–49
Geminoids robots, 129–130

Golden Mean, 41, 62
Goldfein, Jocelyn, 28
Google
    Evans' comment on, 124
    free Internet access from, 120–121
    mobile apps, quality controls, 28
    mobile developer ecosystem at,
        124–125
    mobile platform expansion, 136
    Nest purchased by, 44
    search engine leadership, 22
Google Glass, 75–76, 83, 96
Greene, Robert, 93
GreenOwl Mobile, 8, 45
growth teams, 107

H
Harvard Business School study
    (2011), 88
Hawking, Stephen, 131
health initiatives, mobile, 121
Heidegger, Martin, 131
Her movie (Jonze), 64–65
HomeAway, 25
Hooked (Eyal), 71
hooks, in building for learning, 109
The Human Condition (Arendt),
    131–132
human-first principles
    as basis of mobile products, 9
    body component, 31
    mind component, 32
    spirit component, 31–32

I
Impressionist paintings, 40–41
Inkinen, Sami, 98
Instacart, 24
Instagram
    beauty aspect of, 44, 59–61
    digital advertising on, 15
    Facebook purchase of, 44

Instagram (*continued*)
  integration with Facebook, 60
  smartphone use and, 125–126
  successful app launch, 126
internal filters
  description, 81, 90
  in Facebook, 67, 86–87
  meaning and, 83–84, 147
  people, 84
  place, 83–84
  in Trulia, 81–82
  user personalization and, 147
International Digital Emmy, 3
Internet
  early website history, 19–20
  e-commerce, 20, 120, 126
  global free access effort, 120–121
  mobile book availability, 122
  responsive websites, 15–16, 18–19
  smartphone interactions with, 15,
    50, 100, 120, 132
Internet of Things, 136
Internet.org initiative, 120–121
iPhone
  app launch for, 18
  beauty aspect of, 39, 50–51
  capacitive touch screens, 118
  daily use data, 41
  Internet browsing on, 50
  Jobs' announcement of, 42, 117
  wow factor, 42
  See also Siri

J
Jobs, Steve, 42, 117, 124
Jonze, Spike, 64–65

K
KnockKnock, 49
Kochava, 105
Krishna, Golden, 45
Kuniavsky, Mike, 136

L
Lanier, Jaron, 74
layers, in building for learning, 109,
    110
lean agile (scientific tool), 106
Leanplum, 105
learning
  artistic tools, 109–110
  building for, 104–114
  in context, 102–104
  in Facebook, 112–114
  fast, adapting to us, 95–98
  in Nokia, 110–112
  scientific tools, 104–105, 107–108
  slow, breaking new ground,
    98–102
  by WhatsApp, 97–98
  by Yelp, 101–102
Lehman, Bastian, 24
Lyft
  early challenges, 95
  ease in using app, 70
  power sharers and, 24
  strategy for success, 95–96

M
Mad Men *era, 21*
Mandela, Nelson, 93–94
Mastery (Greene), 93
Mayer, Marissa, 22
McCue, Mike, 47–48
meaning (of mobile products)
  building for, 81–85
  community and, 63, 71–76, 127,
    147
  context of, 76–81
  emotion and, 70
  external filters and, 81, 82, 84–85
  Facebook and, 86–87
  internal filters and, 83–84, 147
  personalization and, 63, 66–71, 90,
    127, 147

Spirit Rule and, 31–32, 33, 37, 63, 80–84
Yelp and, 87–89
millennials
  Body Rule and, 133–135
  as digital natives, 132
  Mind Rule and, 138–140
  Mobile Formula and, 141
  Pew Research Center description, 132
  privacy beliefs of, 75
  shaping of mobile revolution by, 117, 132–141
  smartphone dependency of, 132
  Spirit Rule and, 135–136
mind-body-spirit trilogy. *See* Body Rule; Mind Rule; Spirit Rule
Mind Rule, 91–115
  building for learning, 104–110
  description, 32, 33, 35
  learning fast and, 95–98
  learning in context and, 102–104
  learning slow and, 98–102
  millennials and, 138–140
  relation to mobile products, 13, 36
  scientific/artistic tools, 107–110
  Sonos and, 147
  Uber and, 147
  See also learning
Mixpanel, 105
mobile apps
  Corporate America's demand for, 7
  for dating, 5
  Flurry's industry data, 19
  implied values of, 14
  launching, 18–19
  mobile marketing and, 15
  pre-deployment quality controls, 28–29
  problem-solving role, 94–96
  See also specific mobile apps

mobile-first
  Facebook's transition to, 28, 126
  mind-body-spirit trilogy and, 30
  reasons for becoming, 29–30, 35
  Sonos's transition to, 144, 147
Mobile Formula
  all encompassing quality of, 143
  creation of, 8
  Facebook case study, 126–128
  in the future, 128–141
  human-first principles, 31–33, 36
  millennials and, 141
  in the past, 118–122
  in the present, 122–128
  role in mobile product success, 13
  See also Body Rule; Mind Rule; Spirit Rule
mobile phones
  evolution of, 119–120
  hardware component, 118–122
  reason to buy component, 123–126
mobile revolution
  abundance of data in, 73
  Big Bang theory behind, 118–119
  consequences of ignoring, 20–21
  description, 2–3
  global entrepreneurship and, 122
  hardware component, 118–122
  learning fast and, 95–98
  learning in context and, 102–104
  learning slow and, 98–102
  millennials' shaping of, 117, 132–141
  origin of, 117
  search for formula, 4
  sharing economy and, 23–27, 36
mom test (of beauty), 37, 47–48, 62, 145–146
money services, mobile, 122
Montreal, Canada, smartphone app, 137–138

Mori, Masahiro, 130
Motorola, 4
MS-DOS (Microsoft Disk Operating System), 123–124
Music Genome, of Pandora, 43
Musk, Elon, 131
MyFitnessPal, 7

N
natural language processing, 77–78
Nest, 44
Net Promoter Score (NPS), 102–103, 104
Netscape, 124
New York Times, 93
99designs, 122
Nokia
 building for learning by, 110–112
 connecting people mission of, 120
 dismissal of iPhone technology, 117–118
 early mobile designs, 119
 incubation labs, 3
 mobile market leadership, 3–4, 120
 Opera Software and, 6
 reason to buy component of, 123
 resistive touch screens of, 112
 smartphone success, 3–4
Nokia Life Tools, 121

O
Oculus Rift, 29, 134
Opera Mediaworks, 101
Opera Software
 free Internet access from, 120–121
 mobile video advertising success, 6–7
 success of app, 100–101
operating systems, 123–124
Owyang, Jeremiah, 23

P
Pandora
 choices made by, 10
 Music Genome of, 43
 Sonos speakers linking with, 146
 thumbing and, 43
PayPal, 87
Peers.org, 25
people (internal filter), 84
Periscope, 133–134
permission (external filter), 85
personalization (of mobile products)
 design considerations, 54, 63, 81, 90, 136–137, 144
 emotions and, 80–81
 meaning and, 63, 66–71, 90, 127, 147
 privacy and, 73
 Spirit Rule and, 34, 138
 Tinder and, 66–67
Pew Research Center, 132
Pillow, 25
place filters, 83–84
policy filters, 84–85
popularity filters, 85, 89
Postmates, 22–23
power operators, 24–25
Predictably Irrational (Ariely), 79
privacy
 baby boomers' beliefs on, 75
 community concerns about, 73–75, 90
 external filters and, 82, 84–85
 Google Glass and, 76
 millennials' beliefs on, 75
 Spirit Rule and, 32
Pythagoras, 46

Q
Qualcomm, 136–137
The Question Concerning Technology (Heidegger), 131

Index

R

Rakuten, 103
reason to buy component, of mobile phones, 123–126
responsive websites, 15–16, 18–19
ridesharing services. *See* Lyft; Uber
Robinson, Joe, 50
robotics, 129–130
Rudin, Ken, 105–106

S

Samsung, 4, 136–137
Save the Trees, mobile game, 137
scientific tools, in building for learning
  big data, 105, 106
  description, 104–105
  funnels, 108–109
  goals, 107–108
  growth teams' mastery of, 107
  lean agile, 106
  turnkey solution companies, 105
selective insulation, 100
sharing economy
  definition, 23
  Fordism comparison, 26–27
  job flexibility feature, 25–26
  local delivery services, 22
  mobile revolution and, 23–27, 36
  new entrepreneurs of, 13, 23–27
  Owyang's expertise on, 23
  power operators of, 24–25
  professionalization of, 24
  ridesharing services, 22
shortcuts, in building for learning, 109
Simmons, Russel, 87
Siri, 64, 77–78
Slack, 8, 51–52
smart apparel companies, 21
smartphone dependency, 132
social networks

connectivity study, 72–73
content sharing on, 60
digital advertising on, 15
reluctancy in joining, 99
rise of, 6, 44
See also specific networks
social norms
  community and, 63, 71–76, 90
  external filters and, 82, 85, 147
  Spirit Rule and, 32, 63
Sonos, 145, 146
Sony, 136–137
Spirit Rule, 63–90
  community and, 34
  description, 31–32, 34
  meaning aspect, 31–32, 33, 37, 66–89
  millennials and, 135–136
  relation to mobile products, 13, 36
  Sonos and, 146
  Uber and, 146
  See also personalization (of mobile products)
Stoppelman, Jeremy, 87

T

targeting of new users, 98–99
thumb test
  beauty and, 62
  GreenOwl and, 45
  Pandora and, 43
  product assessment and, 144, 146
  requirements for passing, 42–43, 56
  Uber and, 145
Tinder, 7, 66–68
Tolstoy, Leo, 46, 62
Trulia, 6, 126
  internal filters in, 81–82
  NPS metric, 102–103, 104
Twitter, 15, 133–134

U
Uber
    Body Rule and, 145
    ease in using app, 70
    Mind Rule and, 147
    origin of greatness of, 92
    sharing economy member, 22,
        25–26, 70
    smartphone use and, 125–126
    Spirit Rule and, 146
    successful app launch, 126
UNESCO study of mobile phone use,
    121–122

V
Viber, 8, 103–104
Virtual Human Interaction Lab
    (Stanford University), 134
visions of mobile companies, 92

W
WeChat, 15
What Is Art? (Tolstoy), 46
WhatsApp

    advertising on, 15
    Facebook's purchase of, 29
    learning by, 97–98
    selective insulation by, 100
    smartphone use and, 125–126
    successful app launch, 126
Whirlpool, 136–137

Y
Yahoo, 21–22
Yang, Jerry, 21
Yelp, 8, 126
    external filters in, 87–89
    learning by, 101–102
    trustworthiness of, 89
Your Are Not a Gadget *(Lanier)*, 74

Z
Zillow, 109
Zuckerberg, Mark, 125

About the Author

 SC Moatti is a mobile veteran from Silicon Valley and a recognized thought leader on mobile, innovation and leadership. While serving as an executive at such mobile pioneers as Facebook, Trulia, and Nokia, Moatti launched and monetized mobile products that are now used by billions of people and have received prestigious awards, including an International Digital Emmy Award nomination.

Moatti currently runs Products That Count, an organization that helps businesses of all sizes become mobile. She also serves on the board of Opera Software, a publicly traded mobile giant with over one billion users. She is a lecturer at Stanford University, where she earned her MBA, and has a Masters of Science in electrical engineering.

Her commentaries on mobile products and the mobile revolution can be found at scmoatti.com, the Harvard Business Review, the Huffington Post, and other forums.

A native of Paris, France, SC lives in San Francisco, California. When she isn't working, she enjoys tango, martial arts, and hosting parties.

✸ Berrett–Koehler
<u>BK</u> Publishers

Berrett-Koehler is an independent publisher dedicated to an ambitious mission: *connecting people and ideas to create a world that works for all*.

We believe that to truly create a better world, action is needed at all levels—individual, organizational, and societal. At the individual level, our publications help people align their lives with their values and with their aspirations for a better world. At the organizational level, our publications promote progressive leadership and management practices, socially responsible approaches to business, and humane and effective organizations. At the societal level, our publications advance social and economic justice, shared prosperity, sustainability, and new solutions to national and global issues.

A major theme of our publications is "Opening Up New Space." Berrett-Koehler titles challenge conventional thinking, introduce new ideas, and foster positive change. Their common quest is changing the underlying beliefs, mindsets, institutions, and structures that keep generating the same cycles of problems, no matter who our leaders are or what improvement programs we adopt.

We strive to practice what we preach—to operate our publishing company in line with the ideas in our books. At the core of our approach is stewardship, which we define as a deep sense of responsibility to administer the company for the benefit of all of our "stakeholder" groups: authors, customers, employees, investors, service providers, and the communities and environment around us.

We are grateful to the thousands of readers, authors, and other friends of the company who consider themselves to be part of the "BK Community." We hope that you, too, will join us in our mission.

A BK Business Book

This book is part of our BK Business series. BK Business titles pioneer new and progressive leadership and management practices in all types of public, private, and nonprofit organizations. They promote socially responsible approaches to business, innovative organizational change methods, and more humane and effective organizations.

Berrett–Koehler
Publishers

Connecting people and ideas
to create a world that works for all

Dear Reader,

Thank you for picking up this book and joining our worldwide community of Berrett-Koehler readers. We share ideas that bring positive change into people's lives, organizations, and society.

To welcome you, we'd like to offer you a free e-book. You can pick from among twelve of our bestselling books by entering the promotional code **BKP92E** here: http://www.bkconnection.com/welcome.

When you claim your free e-book, we'll also send you a copy of our e-news-letter, the *BK Communiqué*. Although you're free to unsubscribe, there are many benefits to sticking around. In every issue of our newsletter you'll find

- A free e-book
- Tips from famous authors
- Discounts on spotlight titles
- Hilarious insider publishing news
- A chance to win a prize for answering a riddle

Best of all, our readers tell us, "Your newsletter is the only one I actually read." So claim your gift today, and please stay in touch!

Sincerely,

Charlotte Ashlock
Steward of the BK Website

Questions? Comments? Contact me at bkcommunity@bkpub.com.

Certified

Ⓑ

Corporation
bcorporation.net